PELICAN BOOKS

THE ARCHITECT AND SOCIETY
Edited by John Fleming and Hugh Honour

The aim of this series is to present the great architects, buildings and towns of the world in their social and cultural environments. The series includes *The Architects of the Parthenon* by Rhys Carpenter, *The British Museum* by J. Mordaunt Crook, *Chartres* by George Henderson, *Inigo Jones* by Sir John Summerson, *Palladio* by James Ackerman, and *Christopher Wren* (in hardback only, published by Allen Lane The Penguin Press) by Kerry Downes.

Los Angeles
THE ARCHITECTURE OF FOUR ECOLOGIES

Reyner Banham is Professor of the History of Architecture at University College, London, and he was Director of the undergraduate programme in the School of Environmental Studies there, during 1970–72.

His involvement with Los Angeles began when he was invited to participate in a symposium on historical teaching before the institution of the Urban Design course at the University of California (Los Angeles) in 1965, and he has taught either there or at the University of Southern California for part of each year since. He has now taken a teaching post in Buffalo, New York.

Born in Norwich in 1922, he was originally destined for an engineering career, but he took up the history of art and architecture in 1949, gaining his doctorate in 1958. He joined the editorial staff of *Architectural Review* in 1952 and remained with the magazine until 1964 when he left to undertake the research for his book *Architecture of the Well-tempered Environment*. Other books include *Theory and Design in the First Machine Age* and *The New Brutalism*. He wrote *Reyner Banham Loves Los Angeles* which was shown on BBC Television in 1972. He is also known for his writings on pop art and design, which often appear in the weekly *New Society*. He is married, with two grown-up children.

PENGUIN BOOKS

Los Angeles

The Architecture of Four Ecologies

Reyner Banham

Penguin Books Ltd, Harmondsworth, Middlesex, England
Penguin Books, 625 Madison Avenue, New York, New York 10022, U.S.A.
Penguin Books Australia Ltd, Ringwood, Victoria, Australia
Penguin Books Canada Ltd, 41 Steelcase Road West, Markham, Ontario, Canada
Penguin Books (N.Z.) Ltd, 182–190 Wairau Road, Auckland 10, New Zealand

First published by Allen Lane The Penguin Press 1971
Published in Pelican Books 1973
Reprinted 1976
Copyright © Reyner Banham, 1971

Designed by Gerald Cinamon
Set in Monotype Garamond
Made and printed in Great Britain by
Fletcher & Son Ltd, Norwich

To CEDRIC PRICE who first called upon me to testify in public on LA

Contents

List of Illustrations

Where no source reference is given the photograph has been supplied by the author

Acknowledgements

My thanks are due in the first place to John Fleming, for inquiring if I thought there were the makings of a book in Los Angeles, and if I knew of a possible author for it. . . . Given that initial impetus, my subsequent thanks must go to:

David Gebhard and Esther McCoy for their specialized help and encouragement; George A. Dudley, former Dean, and the rest of the architecture faculty at UCLA, especially Jean King; the Special Collections and Research Libraries at UCLA; Dean Hurst, Crombie Taylor and Randell Makinson at USC; Charles Eames, Craig Ellwood, Pierre Koenig, David Travers, Nathan Shapira, Mel Best, Herbert Kahn, Art Seidenbaum, Rad Sutnar, Jack Roberts, Philip M. Lovell, Judith Ransome Miller, Irving Blum, Ed Ruscha, Mike Salisbury, Joseph LaBarbera of Title Insurance & Trust Company, and John Entenza, but for whom my whole view of Los Angeles might have been very different or non-existent.

Illustrations 3, 5, 34, 39, 79 and 105 drawn by Mary Banham; illustrations 9 and 30 drawn by Paul White.

Views of Los Angeles

On my first visit to Los Angeles I was conventionally prepared for almost anything except for what it really looked like – a quite beautiful place.

Nathan Silver: *New Statesman*, 28 March 1969

Now I know subjective opinions can vary, but personally I reckon LA as the noisiest, the smelliest, the most uncomfortable, and most uncivilised major city in the United States. In short a stinking sewer . . .

Adam Raphael: *Guardian*, 22 July 1968

It is as though London stretched unbroken from St Albans to Southend in a tangle of ten-lane four-deck super parkways, hamburger stands, banks, topless drug-stores, hippie hide-outs, Hiltons, drive-in mortuaries, temples of obscure and extraordinary religions, sinless joy and joyless sin, restaurants built to resemble bowler hats, insurance offices built to resemble Babylon, all shrouded below the famous blanket of acrid and corroding smog.

James Cameron: *Evening Standard*, 9 September 1968

To be able to choose what you want to be and how you want to live, without worrying about social censure, is obviously more important to Angelenos than the fact that they do not have a Piazza San Marco.

Jan Rowan: *Progressive Architecture*, February 1968

Whatever glass and steel monuments may be built downtown, the essence of Los Angeles, its true identifying characteristic, is mobility. Freedom of movement has long given life a special flavour there, liberated the individual to enjoy the sun and space that his environment so abundantly offered, put the manifold advantages of a great metropolitan area within his grasp.

Richard Austin Smith: *Fortune*, March 1965

In Los Angeles people think of space in terms of time, time in terms of routes . . . and of automobiles as natural and essential extensions of themselves . . . Los Angeles has no weather. It rains during February but when it is not raining it is warm and sunny and the palm trees silhouette against the smoggy heat haze sky.

Miles: *International Times*, 14 March 1969

Burn, Baby, burn!

Slogan of the Watts rioters, 1965

LA has beautiful (if man-made) sunsets.

Miles: op. cit.

Los Angeles

1   In the Rear-view Mirror

A city seventy miles square but rarely seventy years deep apart from a small downtown not yet two centuries old and a few other pockets of ancientry, Los Angeles is instant architecture in an instant townscape. Most of its buildings are the first and only structures on their particular parcels of land; they are couched in a dozen different styles, most of them imported, exploited, and ruined within living memory. Yet the city has a comprehensible, even consistent, quality to its built form, unified enough to rank as a fit subject for an historical monograph.

Historical monograph? Can such an old-world, academic, and precedent-laden concept claim to embrace so unprecedented a human phenomenon as this city of Our Lady Queen of the Angels of Porciuncula? – otherwise known as Internal Combustion City, Surfurbia, Smogville, Aerospace City, Systems Land, the Dream-factory of the Western world. It's a poor historian who finds any human artefact alien to his professional capacities, a poorer one who cannot find new bottles for new wine. In any case, the new wine of Angeleno architecture has already been decanted into one of the older types of historical bottle with a success that I will not even try to emulate.

Architecture in Southern California by David Gebhard and Robert Winter is a model version of the classical type of architectural gazetteer – erudite, accurate, clear, well-mapped, pocket-sized. No student of the architecture of Los Angeles can afford to stir out of doors without it. But there is no need to try and write it again; all I wish to do here is to record my profound and fundamental debt to the authors, and echo their admission of even more fundamental indebtedness – to Esther McCoy and her 'one-woman crusade' to get Southern California's modern architectural history recorded and its monuments appreciated.

1. Chaos on Echo Park

Yet even the professed intention of Gebhard and Winter to cover 'a broad cross-section of the varieties of Angeleno architecture', is inhibited by the relatively conventional implicit definition of 'architecture' accepted by these open-minded observers; their spectrum includes neither hamburger bars and other Pop ephemeridae at one extreme, nor freeway structures and other civil engineering at the other. However, both are as crucial to the human ecologies and built environments of Los Angeles as are dated works in classified styles by named architects.

In order to accommodate such extremes, the chapters that follow will have to deviate from accepted norms for architectural histories of cities. What I have aimed to do is to present the architecture (in a fairly conventional sense of the word) within the topographical and historical context of the total artefact that constitutes Greater Los Angeles, because it is this double context that binds the polymorphous architectures into a comprehensible unity that cannot often be discerned by comparing monument with monument out of context.

So when most observers report monotony, not unity, and within that monotony, confusion rather than variety, this is usually because the context has escaped them [1]; and it has escaped them because it is unique (like all the best unities) and without any handy terms of comparison. It is difficult to register the total artefact as a distinctive human construct because there is nothing else with which to compare it, and thus no class into which it may be pigeonholed. And we historians are too prone to behave like Socrates in Paul Valéry's *Eupalinos*, to reject the inscrutable, to hurl the unknown in the ocean.

How then to bridge this gap of comparability. One can most properly begin by learning the local language; and the language of design, architecture, and urbanism in Los Angeles is the language of movement. Mobility outweighs monumentality there to a unique degree, as Richard Austin Smith pointed out in a justly famous article in 1965, and the city will never be fully understood by those who cannot move fluently through its diffuse urban texture, cannot go with the flow of its unprecedented life. So, like earlier generations of English intellectuals who taught themselves Italian in order to read Dante in the original, I learned to drive in order to read Los Angeles in the original.

But whereas knowledge of Dante's tongue could serve in reading other Italian texts, full command of Angeleno dynamics qualifies one only to read Los Angeles, the uniquely mobile metropolis. Again that word 'uniquely' . . . I make no apology for it. The splendours and miseries of Los Angeles, the graces and grotesqueries, appear to me as unrepeatable as they are unprecedented. I share neither the optimism of those who see Los Angeles as the prototype of all future cities, nor the gloom of those who see it as the harbinger of universal urban doom. Once the history of the city is brought under review, it is immediately apparent that no city has ever been produced by such an extraordinary mixture of geography, climate, economics, demography, mechanics and culture; nor is it likely that an even remotely similar mixture will ever occur again. The interaction of these factors needs to be kept in constant historical view – and since it is manifestly dangerous to face backwards while at the steering wheel, the common metaphor of history as the rear-view mirror of civilization seems necessary, as well as apt, in any study of Los Angeles.

First, observe an oddity in the 'Yellow Pages' of the local phone books; many firms list, in the same size type and without comment, branches in Hawaii, New Zealand, and Australia. This is neither a picturesque curiosity nor commercial bragging – it is simply the next natural place to have branches, a continuation of the great westward groundswell of population that brought the Angelenos to the Pacific shore in the first place, a groundswell that can still be felt throughout the life of the city.

Los Angeles looks naturally to the Sunset, which can be stunningly handsome, and named one of its great boulevards after that favourite evening view. But if the eye follows the sun, westward migration cannot. The Pacific beaches are where young men stop going West, where the great waves of agrarian migration from Europe and the Middle West broke in a surf of fulfilled and frustrated hopes. The strength and nature of this westward flow need to be understood; it underlies the differences of mind between Los Angeles and its sister-metropolis to the north.

San Francisco was plugged into California from the sea; the Gold Rush brought its first population and their culture round Cape Horn;

their prefabricated Yankee houses and prefabricated New England (or European) attitudes were dumped unmodified on the Coast. Viewed from Southern California it looks like a foreign enclave, like the Protestant Pale in Ireland, because the Southern Californians came, predominantly, overland to Los Angeles, slowly traversing the whole North American land-mass and its evolving history.

They brought with them – and still bring – the prejudices, motivations, and ambitions of the central heartland of the USA. The first major wave of immigration came from Kansas City on excursion tickets after 1885; later they came in second-hand cars out of the dust-bowl – not for nothing is Mayor Yorty known (behind his back) as the Last of the Okies, and Long Beach as the Main Seaport of Iowa! In one unnervingly true sense, Los Angeles is the Middle West raised to flash-point, the authoritarian dogmas of the Bible Belt and the perennial revolt against them colliding at critical mass under the palm trees. Out of it comes a cultural situation where only the extreme is normal, and the Middle Way is just the unused reservation down the centre of the Freeway.

Yet these extremes contrive to co-exist with only sporadic flares of violence – on Venice Beach, in Watts, or whatever is the fashionable venue for confrontations. Miraculously the city's extremes include an excessive tolerance. Partly this is that indifference which is Los Angeles's most publicized vice, but it is also a heritage from the extraordinary cultural mixture with which the city began. If Los Angeles is not a monolithic Protestant moral tyranny – and it notoriously is not! – it is because the Mid-western agrarian culture underwent a profound transformation as it hit the coast, a sun-change that pervades moral postures, political attitudes, ethnic groupings, and individual psychologies. This change has often been observed, and usually with bafflement, yet one observer has bypassed the bafflement and gone straight to an allegory of Californiation that seems to hold good from generation to generation – Ray Bradbury in the most fundamental of his Martian stories, *Dark they were and Golden Eyed*, where the earth-family are subtly transformed, even against their wills, into tall, bronzed, gold-eyed Martians who abandon their neat Terran cities and the earthly cares and duty they symbolize, and run free in the mountains.

In one sense, this Martian transformation was forced upon the arriving agriculturalists by their daily occupations. Whereas a wheat-farming family relocating itself in the Central Valley, around Stockton in mid California, might expect to continue wheat-farming, those who went to Southern California could hardly hope even to try. Where water was available, Mediterranean crops made better sense and profit, olives, vines and – above all – citrus fruits, the first great source of wealth in Southern California after land itself. Horny-handed followers of the plough and reaper became gentlemen horticulturalists among their 'groves and fountains'.

The basic plants and crops for this transformed rural culture were already established on the land before the Mid-westerners and North Europeans arrived, for the great wave of westward migration broke across the backwash of a receding wave from the south – the collapsing Mexican regime that was in itself the successor to the original Spanish

2. The pueblo of Los Angeles in 1857

colonization of California. The two currents swirled together around some very substantial Hispanic relics: the Missions, where the fathers had introduced the grape, olive, and orange as well as Christianity, the military communication line of the Camino Real and the Presidio forts, the very Pueblo de Nuestra Señora Reina de Los Angeles de Porciuncula [2].

And, above all, a system of ranching whose large scale, open-handedness and al fresco style were infectious, and whose pattern of land-holding still gives the ultimate title to practically every piece of land in Greater Los Angeles. Most of the original titles granted by the kings of Spain and by the Mexican governors were confirmed by patents granted by the US after 1848 (often a long while after; land-grant litigation became almost a national sport in California) and thus bequeathed to the area a pattern of property lines, administrative boundaries, and place-names [3] that guarantee a kind of cultural immortality to the Hispanic tradition.

So the predominantly Anglo-Saxon culture of Los Angeles ('Built by the British, financed by the Canadians') is deeply entangled with remnants of Spain, and has been so ever since an early arriving *Yanqui* like Benjamin Wilson could translate himself into a 'Don Benito' by marrying into the Yorba clan, and thus into a ranching empire that spread over vast acreages to the east of the Pueblo. This ancient entanglement is still deeply felt, even if it is not officially institutionalized (as in the Spanish *Fiesta* in Santa Barbara, up the coast). It still provides psychological support for the periodical out-bursts of pantiled roofs, adobe construction, arcaded courtyards, that constitute the elusive but ever-present Spanish Colonial Revival style, in all its variants from the simplest stuccoed shed to fantasies of fully-fledged Neo-Churrigueresque [4]. Such architecture should never be brushed off as mere fancy-dress; in Los Angeles it makes both ancestral and environmental sense, and much of the best modern architecture there owes much to its example.

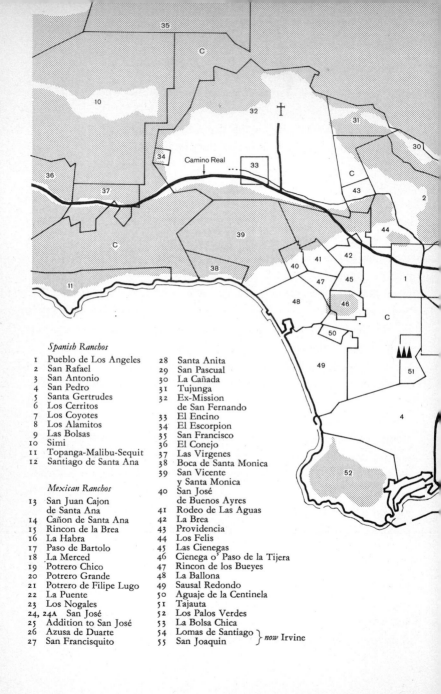

35

C

10

32

†

31

30

34

Camino Real
↓

33

36

C

43

37

2

44

39

40 41 42

47 45

38

48 46

C

11

50

49

51

Spanish Ranchos

1	Pueblo de Los Angeles
2	San Rafael
3	San Antonio
4	San Pedro
5	Santa Gertrudes
6	Los Cerritos
7	Los Coyotes
8	Los Alamitos
9	Las Bolsas
10	Simi
11	Topanga-Malibu-Sequit
12	Santiago de Santa Ana

Mexican Ranchos

13	San Juan Cajon de Santa Ana
14	Cañon de Santa Ana
15	Rincon de la Brea
16	La Habra
17	Paso de Bartolo
18	La Merced
19	Potrero Chico
20	Potrero Grande
21	Potrero de Filipe Lugo
22	La Puente
23	Los Nogales
24, 24A	San José
25	Addition to San José
26	Azusa de Duarte
27	San Francisquito

28	Santa Anita
29	San Pascual
30	La Cañada
31	Tujunga
32	Ex-Mission de San Fernando
33	El Encino
34	El Escorpion
35	San Francisco
36	El Conejo
37	Las Virgenes
38	Boca de Santa Monica
39	San Vicente y Santa Monica
40	San José de Buenos Ayres
41	Rodeo de Las Aguas
42	La Brea
43	Providencia
44	Los Felis
45	Las Cienegas
46	Cienega o' Paso de la Tijera
47	Rincon de los Bueyes
48	La Ballona
49	Sausal Redondo
50	Aguaje de la Centinela
51	Tajauta
52	Los Palos Verdes
53	La Bolsa Chica
54	Lomas de Santiago
55	San Joaquin

54, 55 } *now* Irvine

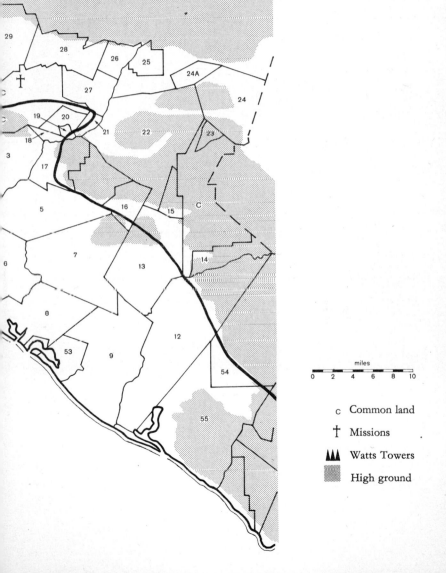

3. Map of Spanish and
Mexican Ranchos

miles

0 2 4 6 8 10

c Common land

† Missions

▲▲▲ Watts Towers

High ground

4. St Vincent's church, 1923, Albert C. Martin, architect

As this architecture shows, the mixture of Hispanic and Anglo-Saxon traditions could have provided the basis for an interesting culture, even if its economic basis had remained agrarian. But the Yankees were coming because they knew a better trick with land than just ranching it; they stormed in on the crest of a wave of technological self-confidence and entrepreneurial abandon that left simple ranching little hope of survival. Land was acquired from the grant holders by every means in the rule book and some outside it, was subdivided, watered, put down to intensive cropping, and ultimately offered as residential plots in a landscape that must have appeared to anyone from east of the Rockies like an earthly Paradise.

Whatever man has done subsequently to the climate and environment of Southern California, it remains one of the ecological wonders of the habitable world. Given water to pour on its light and otherwise almost desert soil, it can be made to produce a reasonable facsimile of Eden. Some of the world's most spectacular gardens are in Los Angeles, where the southern palm will literally grow next to northern conifers, and it was this promise of an ecological miracle that was the area's first really saleable product – the 'land of perpetual spring'.

But to produce instant Paradise you have to add water – and keep on adding it. Once the scant local sources had been tapped, wasted, and spoiled, the politics of hydrology became a pressing concern, even a deciding factor in fixing the political boundaries of Los Angeles. The City annexed the San Fernando Valley, murdered the Owens Valley in its first great raid on hinterland waters under William Mulholland, and its hydrological frontier is now on the Colorado River. Yet fertile watered soil is no use if it is inaccessible; transportation was to be the next great shaper of Los Angeles after land and water. From the laying of the first railway down to the port at Wilmington just over a century ago, transport has been an obsession that grew into a way of life [5].

Lines were hardly laid before commuting began along them; scattered communities were joined in a diffuse and unprecedented super-community, whose empty interstices filled up with further townships, vineyards, orchards, health resorts, and the fine tracery of the second generation of railroads – the inter-urbans. By 1910 when amalgamations

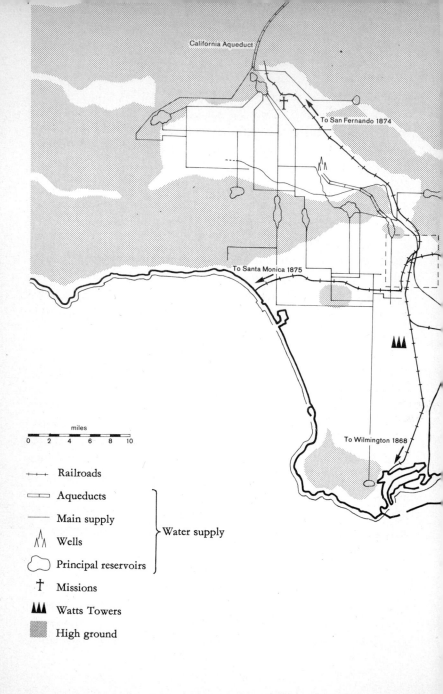

California Aqueduct

To San Fernando 1874

To Santa Monica 1875

To Wilmington 1868

miles
0 2 4 6 8 10

┼┼┼ Railroads

▭ Aqueducts

⎫
Main supply   │
│
Λ∧ Wells   ├ Water supply
∧   │
⌒ Principal reservoirs   │
⎭

✝ Missions

▲▲▲ Watts Towers

░ High ground

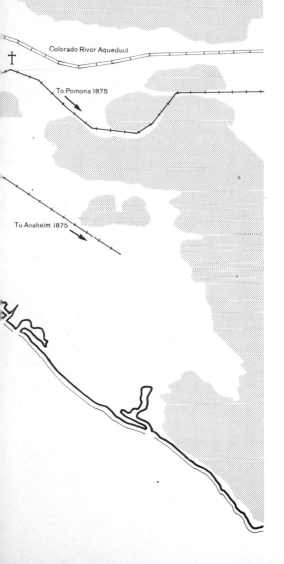

5. Map of the first five railways
out of the pueblo,
and the water-distribution grid
as existing

Colorado River Aqueduct

To Pomona 1875

To Anaheim 1875

and rationalizations had unified these inter-urban commuter lines into the Pacific Electric Railway, the map of its network was a detailed sketch for the whole Los Angeles that exists today. In part this must have been due to the way in which any major investment in transport tends to stabilize a new pattern more permanent than the old one which was disrupted by the investment, but it must have been at least equally due to the coincidence in time of the construction of the PE and a new phase of economic and industrial development.

In the decades on either side of 1900 the economic basis of Angeleno life was transformed. While land and field-produce remained the established basis of wealth, an important new primary industry was added – oil. Its existence had been long known from the natural seepages at the La Brea tar-pits in what is now Hancock Park, but commercial working did not begin until the mid-nineties and large-scale exploitation grew throughout the first quarter of the present century as new fields were discovered. Nowadays drilling rigs or nodding pumps are liable to be found almost anywhere on the plains or along the coast, and the olfactory evidence of the existence of the oil industry is as ubiquitous as the visual.

In those same years of the full florescence of the Pacific Electric, Los Angeles also acquired a major secondary industry and a most remarkable tertiary. The secondary was its port. There had always been harbour facilities on its coast, but the building of the Point Fermin breakwater to enclose the harbour at Wilmington/San Pedro from 1899 onwards was in good time to catch the greatly expanded trade promoted by the opening of the short sea-route from coast to coast through the Panama Canal after 1914. Within the breakwater now are a spreading complex of artificial islands and basins that constitute the largest man-made harbour in the world, clearing three billion dollars worth of goods a year.

And in 1910, the tertiary industry that sets Los Angeles apart even from other cities that now possess the same tertiary, was founded, when the first Hollywood movie was made in a barn at the corner of Sunset and Gower. The movies seem to have been the great imponderable in the history of the area; their economic consequences were undoubtedly great, but it was mad money that the film industry brought in, and in any case it is the cultural consequences that now seem most important. Hollywood brought to Los Angeles an unprecedented and unrepeatable population of genius, neurosis, skill, charlatanry, beauty, vice, talent, and plain old eccentricity, and it brought that population in little over two decades, not the long centuries that most metropolitan cities have required to accumulate a cultured and leisured class. So Hollywood was also the end of innocence and provincialism – the movies found Los Angeles a diffuse fruit-growing super-village of some eight hundred thousand souls, and handed it over to the infant television industry in 1950 a world metropolis of over four million.

Now all these economic and cultural developments tended to go with the flow of urbanization that the Pacific Electric both served and stimulated. Oil was struck all over the area, the harbour was spatially expansive and promoted other developments in the south of the central plain, Hollywood populated the foothills and established colonies as far afield as Malibu, while its need for vast areas of studio space indoors and out made it almost a major land-user on sites ever further from Sunset Boulevard.

The motor age, from the mid-twenties onwards, again tended to confirm the going pattern, and the freeway network that now traverses the city, which has since added major aerospace industries to its economic armoury, conspicuously parallels the five first railways out of the pueblo. Indeed the freeways seem to have fixed Los Angeles in canonical and monumental form, much as the great streets of Sixtus V fixed Baroque Rome, or the *Grands Travaux* of Baron Haussmann fixed the Paris of *la belle époque*. Whether you regard them as crowns of thorns or chaplets of laurels, the freeways are what the tutelary deity of the City of Angels should wear upon her head instead of the mural crowns sported by civic goddesses of old.

But while we drive along the freeways that are its crowning glory or prime headache, and con the rear-view mirror for historical illumination, what shall be our route? Simply to go from the oldest monument to the newest could well prove a short, boring and uninstructive journey, because the point about this giant city, which has grown almost simultaneously all over, is that all its parts are equal and equally accessible from all other parts at once. Everyday commuting tends less and less to move by the classic systole and diastole in and out of downtown, more and more to move by an almost random or Brownian motion over the whole area. The chapters that follow are intended to invite the reader to do the same; only the history of modern architecture is treated in anything like chronological order, and can be read in historical sequence. The rest is to be visited at the reader's choice or fancy, with that freedom of movement that is the prime symbolic attribute of the Angel City.

2   Ecology I: Surfurbia

The Beaches are what other metropolises should envy in Los Angeles, more than any other aspect of the city. From Malibu to Balboa almost continuous white sand beach runs for seventy-odd miles, nearly all of it open to public access, much less of it encroached upon by industry than alarmist literature might lead one to suppose, though at one or two points considerable vigilance will be required for years to come – the sea is too handy a dumping ground for cost-cutting industries and public 'services'. But such worries notwithstanding, Los Angeles is the greatest City-on-the-Shore in the world; its only notable rival, in fact, is Rio de Janeiro (though the open ocean-beaches of Los Angeles are preferable in many ways) and its only rival in potential is, probably, Perth, Western Australia.

Historically this situation is entirely apt. In the long view of geological time, Los Angeles has only recently emerged from the ocean; most of what is now the Greater Los Angeles basin was below sea-level in Jurassic times, and has been hoisted into the sunshine by a prolonged geological lifting process, that has marked the flanks of Palos Verdes mountain [6] with as many as thirteen superimposed

6. The Beach Cities from Palos Verdes mountain

benches or terraces marking ancient beach levels. Palos Verdes is indeed believed to be the fastest-rising piece of land on the earth's surface, and the proneness of the whole area to earthquakes and minor tremors is proverbial.

But Los Angeles is not a seaside city in the classical mould. It was not entered or conquered from the sea, nor was it for a long time a port of consequence. It was an inland foundation that suddenly began to leap-frog to the sea in the railway age, establishing on the shoreline sub-cities that initiated its peculiar pattern of many-centred growth. Angelenos (and others) hurried down to the beaches for health and recreation, then decided to stay when they discovered the railways had made it possible to commute to work-places inland. The date of change-over from resort status to that of residential suburb can be identified by a variety of techniques:

'My brother, who is in the piano-business, tells me that Santa Monica uses more pianos than any other city of its size in the County. That means that Santa Monica has indeed become a home city, and is no longer simply a summer or winter pleasure resort,' wrote Marshall Breeden in 1925 of the prototype of all Angeleno beach cities, and this has been the pattern all along the shore.

But an air of health and pleasure still attaches to the beaches, partly for good physiological reasons, and partly because the cultivation and cult of the physical man (and woman) is obviously a deeply ingrained trait in the psychology of Southern California. Sun, sand, and surf are held to be ultimate and transcendental values, beyond mere physical goods:

'Give me a beach, something to eat, and a couple of broads, and I can get along without material things,' said a Santa Monica bus-driver to me, summing up a very widespread attitude in which the pleasures of physical well-being are not 'material' in the sense of the pleasures of possessing goods and chattels. The culture of the beach is in many ways a symbolic rejection of the values of the consumer society, a place where a man needs to own only what he stands up in – usually a pair of frayed shorts and sun-glasses.

There is a sense in which the beach is the only place in Los Angeles where all men are equal and on common ground. There appears to be (and to a varying degree there really is) a real alternative to the tendency of life to compartmentalize in this freemasonry of the beaches, and although certain high schools allegedly maintain a 'turf' system that recognizes certain beaches as the private territories of particular schools, it is roughly speaking possible for a man in beach trunks and a girl in a bikini to go to almost any beach unmolested – even private ones if they can muster the nerve to walk in. One way and another, the beach is what life is all about in Los Angeles.

For the purpose of the present study, that beach runs from the Malibu strip at the western extremity to the Balboa peninsula in the south, and is marked by a distinguished modern building at either end: Craig Ellwood's Hunt house of 1955 [7] at Malibu, and Rudolph

7. Hunt house, Malibu, 1955, Craig Ellwood, architect

Schindler's epoch-making Lovell house of thirty years earlier at Newport Beach, where the Balboa peninsula begins. Between the two the beach varies in structure, format, orientation, social status, age of development, and whatnot, but remains continuously The Beach.

At Malibu the beach is private; not because antisocial upper-class elements covered it with restrictive legislation, but because the pattern of development makes it physically inaccessible. From Malibu pier east to Santa Monica pier, the great arterial highway of the Beach Cities, the Pacific Coast Highway, is squeezed between sand cliffs to the landward, and the beach itself. Between the highway and the beach, what were once sold as small plots of land for beach-huts are now continuously covered by sizeable middle-class houses [8a, b] in such

8a, b. Beach, houses and highway, Malibu

close contiguity that for miles there is no way to squeeze between them and get to the beach, which thus becomes a secluded communal back-yard for the inhabitants. This situation is not absolute; there are sizeable inserts of public beach towards Santa Monica, but for miles through Malibu the houses make a continuous street-front behind which the sea is their private preserve [9].

Not only is this pattern opened up by public beaches towards Santa Monica, but human occupation in the landward side changes too, and

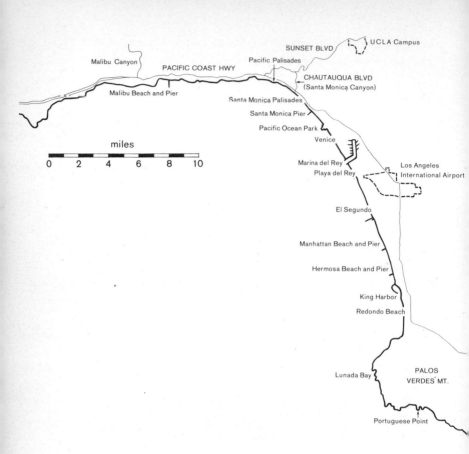

miles

0 2 4 6 8 10

Malibu Canyon

PACIFIC COAST HWY

Malibu Beach and Pier

SUNSET BLVD

UCLA Campus

Pacific Palisades

CHAUTAUQUA BLVD
(Santa Monica Canyon)

Santa Monica Palisades

Santa Monica Pier

Pacific Ocean Park

Venice

Marina del Rey

Playa del Rey

Los Angeles
International Airport

El Segundo

Manhattan Beach and Pier

Hermosa Beach and Pier

King Harbor

Redondo Beach

Lunada Bay

PALOS
VERDES MT.

Portuguese Point

9. Map of the Los Angeles beaches

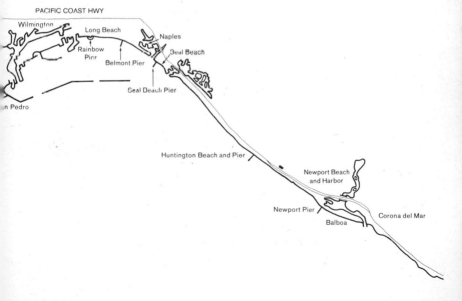

PACIFIC COAST HWY

Wilmington

Long Beach

Naples

Rainbow
Pier

Seal Beach

Belmont Pier

Seal Beach Pier

n Pedro

Huntington Beach and Pier

Newport Beach
and Harbor

Newport Pier

Corona del Mar

Balboa

10. Santa Monica Canyon, *c.* 1870

some major canyon roads come down to the coast highway. Geographically the most important of these is Chautauqua Boulevard, which not only provides a short-cut between Sunset Boulevard and the sea, but actually reaches the coast at the mouth of Santa Monica Canyon. Though it now has the relatively new and planned community of Pacific Palisades on the slopes behind it, the importance of Santa Monica Canyon [10] is that it is the point where Los Angeles first came to the Beaches. From the garden of Charles Eames's house in Pacific Palisades, one can look down on a collection of roofs and roads [11] that cover the old camp-site to which Angelenos started to come for long weekend picnics under canvas from the beginning of the 1870s. The journey from downtown could take two days, so it was not an excursion to be lightly undertaken, but there was soon enough traffic

11. Santa Monica Canyon from the garden of the Eames house

to justify a regular stage-run, and a semi-permanent big tent that served as a dance-hall and could sleep thirty people overnight. In the 1890s the long jetty of 'Port Los Angeles' took the railroad out to deep water hereabouts to unload coal, but the final establishment of Los Angeles' 'official' harbour at San Pedro, plus the discovery that steam locomotives could burn locally drilled oil, wiped out Santa Monica's last attempt to become a major port.

It was an earlier attempt to create such a port that really put Santa Monica in communication with inland Los Angeles. Within a few years of the discovery of the canyon mouth as a picnic beach, the railway had hit the shore at Santa Monica, but on the southern side of the flat-topped mesa on which most of the present Santa Monica stands. Along the top of the bluff where the mesa meets the sea is the

12. Santa Monica Palisades

splendid cliff-top park [12] of Santa Monica Palisades, and behind it there have always been high-class hotels as long as there has been a Santa Monica.

The most senior of the beach cities, 'San Mo' has probably the most distinctive civic atmosphere – though I would be hard put to define it – which can be sensed back inland almost as far as the UCLA campus. Partly it is the generous planning of the street-widths, partly it is the provision of a very good municipal bus service, but chiefly it is having been on the ground long enough to develop an independent personality. The railway that failed to make it a great port nevertheless got it started as a resort city well before most of the others were even a twinkle in a realtor's eye.

South along the beaches, the immediately succeeding cities are much less stylish. Venice, intended to be the most stylish of the lot, was overrun by oil drilling and is now a long uncertain strip of frame houses of varying ages, vacant lots, oil-pumps, and sad gravel scrub. It has the charm of decay, but this will almost certainly disappear in the redevelopments that must follow the creation of the Yacht Harbor inland behind Venice. South of the harbour's mouth (corresponding roughly to the outfall of the old Ballena creek) a low cliff rises in contrast to the flatness of Venice – another mesa, this time topped by Los Angeles International Airport.

And under the flight-path of the jet-liners as they take off to seawards lie the Beach Cities that, unlike old San Mo, correspond most nearly to the surfside way of Angeleno life: Playa del Rey, El Segundo, Manhattan Beach, Hermosa Beach [13], Redondo Beach. These canonical 'surfurbs' are largely the creation of coastwise inter-urban electric railways, whose rusting remains could still be found behind Hermosa Beach, with a crumbling terminus depot at Redondo, when I first began

13. Hermosa Beach

to explore the area. The true beach strip, up to four or five streets deep, lay between the tracks and the sand. The ground is often steep, with little cross-streets plunging sharply between the cottagey houses and small stucco-box stores to the concrete 'board-walk' that characterizes mile after mile of the true surfurbian shore.

This beachside walk is the true artery of the beach life. Closed to wheeled traffic, except public service vehicles such as police cars, life-guard trucks, and the little rubber-tyred trams that run along the

14. Surf-board art

equivalent walks in Santa Monica and Venice, this is the preserve of the pedestrian – including the pedal-cyclist who counts as a pedestrian according to normal US practice. On the inland side it may be lined with private houses, the odd hotel, hamburger bars or even restaurants; on the seaward side usually a low wall to restrain the sand, but also ideal for displaying the torso or servicing scuba gear and surf-boards.

The surf-board is the prime symbolic and functional artefact of these beaches where California surfing began. The sport was brought here – like almost everything else – by the Pacific Electric Railroad in 1907 when, in order to stimulate flagging passenger traffic at weekends, they brought George Freeth, the Hiberno-Hawaiian pioneer surfer, to Redondo Beach to give demonstrations of surf-riding. It remained a tough and restricted sport – largely because of the unwieldy massive wooden boards – until the middle 1950s, when the modern type of board made of plastic foam jacketed in fibreglass hit the surf, handier and effectively cheaper (because mass-produced) than the traditional board. What has happened since is – as they say – history, but few episodes of seaside history since the Viking invasions can have been so colourful. Leaning on the sea-wall or stuck in the sand like plastic megaliths, they concentrate practically the whole capacity of Los Angeles to create stylish decorative imagery [14], and to fix those images with all the panoply of modern visual and material techniques – and all, remember, in the service of the preferred local form of noble savage, pitting his nearly naked muscles and skilled reactions against the full force of the 'mighty hulking Pacific Ocean'.

Southward the run of surfing cities breaks with the irruption of the Palos Verdes mountain, a massive promontory crowned by exclusive residential suburbs and in parts thickly wooded with deliberately planted trees. Its coastline is spectacularly craggy, boasts a few famous beaches like Lunada, and a few very odd monuments, like Marineland of the Pacific, and Lloyd Wright's expressionistic, but very effective glass Wayfarer's Chapel [15], now so overgrown both without and

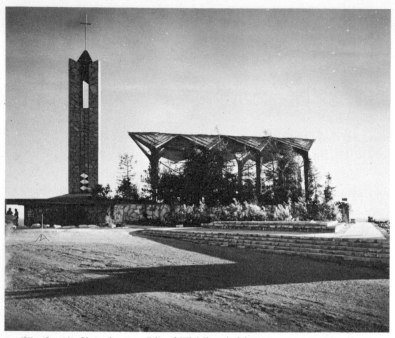

15. Wayfarer's Chapel, 1949, Lloyd Wright, architect

within that it is becoming more of a shrine to fecund nature than to the
Swedenborgian rite. From the eastern face of Palos Verdes mountain
one can look far across San Pedro and the wharves and basins of the
harbour. Largely the invention of Phineas Banning in the early 1860s,
the harbour twice nearly went to Santa Monica, but after some vicious
infighting between railroad interests, the primacy of San Pedro/
Wilmington was confirmed by a Federal Bill appropriating almost three
million dollars for the construction of a major deep-water port there,
and work began on the two-mile sea wall to protect it in 1899.

The other harbour city, on the other bank of the re-routed, tamed
and channelled Los Angeles River, is Long Beach – again mostly a

creation of the Pacific Electric. For a mile or so east from the river mouth it has a rather solid, almost European-style sea front, though the off-shore oil-rigs, beautified with palm-trees and architectural camouflage [16], soon disabuse the visitor of any notion that he is not

16. Beautified oil-rigs off Long Beach

in Southern California. But further east, the normal kind of beachside development reappears and runs on to the end of the sand-spit that encloses Alamitos bay at the mouth of the San Gabriel River. Eastward and southward still lies the tidy municipality of Seal Beach, where they have recently torn up the rail tracks in the central reservation of Electric Avenue – a street name that reveals a common ancestry with most of the other beach cities.

Beyond this, the oil industry reasserts itself. Right down to Huntington Beach (named after the Pacific Electric's founder) new wells and abandoned wells, capped wells and wells straddled by nodding pumps, seem almost as numerous as human habitations and for one incredible mile or so, the Pacific Coast Highway is lined with a double file of pumps standing shoulder to shoulder behind a token 'beautification' fence, their orange painted 'heads' nodding tirelessly and slowly, and always out of synchronization with one another, so that they seem like a herd of extra-terrestrial animals with inscrutable minds of their own.

Huntington Beach, when it is finally reached, is another loosely developed surfers' paradise, marked architecturally by the Huntington Pacific Apartment Community and a famous pier. The Huntington Pacific is a massive development in the now fashionable Kasbah/ Italian-village manner (by Pereira Associates and Leland King Associates) with vaguely Mission-style detailing, perched on the shore over two decks of car-parking. It is a harmless enough piece of tame

17. Huntington Beach Pier

fantasy architecture, but it is literally perched *on the shore,* is surrounded by a wall and is guarded by a uniformed *cop.* If it heralds the subdivision of the shoreline (presumably as oil-leases fall in) into a series of fortified private segments, it is a sorry portent for surfurbia.

Huntington Beach Pier [17], on the other hand, is one of the constituent monuments of the surfing life, the best viewing point and outstanding hazard of the surfing championships, so well known that to ask for 'HBP' will usually find it. The reputations of the piers are understandably functional, rather than architectural, but the whole class of piers must be saluted here as the most characteristic structures in Surfurbia. The beaches are uncommonly well provided with public piers, whether commercially or municipally operated – Malibu, Santa

18. Santa Monica Pier

Monica, Pacific Ocean Park, Venice, Manhattan Beach, the elaborately loop-planned Redondo Pier, Long Beach municipal, Seal Beach, HBP itself, Newport, and Balboa. Some were built for commercial purposes and for fishing, most are simply resort facilities – Seal Beach pier was built by the Bayside Land Company when their piece of the Bolsa Chica rancho was subdivided, but by 1937 it was in such poor condition after the winter storms that it was rebuilt by the municipality, and the city engineer has his name on a bronze plate at the entrance.

But these southern municipal piers are rather simple in their functions. Santa Monica [18], by contrast, is rich and complex and blatantly commercial, a little Luna Park, complete with off-shore parking lots, shops, restaurants and a famous enclosed carousel with apartments for rent in its corner turrets, and Charlie Chaplin used to eat at a famous restaurant near the end of the pier in his early Hollywood days. My own preferred off-shore restaurant is on Redondo pier, which performs the unusual manoeuvre of going out to sea and looping back to the shore, and is currently being developed as a major beachside tourist shopping centre and a rather pleasant pedestrian precinct. And if anyone sought a major monument to the heartbreak that ends the Angeleno dream, there was always Pacific Ocean Park [19], a recent fantasy in stucco and every known style of architecture and human ecology (including a giant artificial rock at the seaward end), a magnificent set of rides and diversions, now demolished after years of bankruptcy . . .

But back to Huntington Beach and southward still; an unresolved area with a big motel, sparse development, then the finest of all the beachside electric generating stations, industrial architecture at its naked best – and for this there may be a good reason in the fact that the steel work was detailed for the Bechtel Corporation who built it, by ex-students of Mies van der Rohe's from Chicago. By day it is a monument in grey steel, by night a fantastic city of lights that can be seen for miles along the shore. Beyond this point, the ecology finally begins to resolve itself into the rich beachside suburbs of Newport Beach, Balboa,

19. Dereliction at Pacific Ocean Park

and Corona del Mar. Substantial houses and apartment blocks serving two-yacht families cluster tight around Newport Harbor; Schindler's Lovell house and other relatively modest residences look out across the Beach, and inland rise the low hills of the Irvine Ranch. This is the end of Surfurbia, marked by two basic facts: firstly that this was as far as the Pacific Electric Railway came along the shore, and if that were not final enough, the Irvine Ranch, undeveloped until less than a decade ago, and still not open to 'normal' subdivision, has always been the traditional barrier to the growth of Los Angeles in this direction. The topography changes as the Irvine lands rise above the flats of the Orange County shore, but more than this the style, the very atmosphere changes. As you cross the Pacific Coast Highway bridge between Newport and Corona del Mar, you know you are leaving Los Angeles.

20. The Lopez adobe, 1878

3   Architecture I: Exotic Pioneers

Modern architecture in Los Angeles started with the useful advantage that the difference between indoors and out was never as clearly defined there, nor as defensive, as it had been in Europe, or was forced to be in other parts of the USA. Traditions inherited from the Rancho period encouraged a tendency to 'speak in superlatives, to live out-of-doors, to tell tall tales, to deal in real estate, to believe what isn't true, to throw dignity out the window, to dress dramatically, and, last but not least, to tackle the impossible'. Lee Shippey's list of old California customs contains other items besides, but these seem to be curiously relevant to what has happened to architecture in Los Angeles, and the lack of distinction between indoors and out sums it up.

Early pictures of the pueblo, whether taken by hand or camera, agree in showing a settlement composed of flat-roofed single-storey adobe buildings with walled courtyards behind, and covered verandas (locally porches) in front, behind, or both, and surviving adobes of Southern California, though mostly equipped with an upper storey, continue this theme – the massive walls and small windows required for one sort of sun-protection are set off by open porches [20] to catch the breezes, as an alternative way of keeping down sun heat.

More recent developments have tended to play up the porches to the point where walls seem almost irrelevant, and concepts of front and back dissolve because there are no façades to attach them to; as Denise Scott-Brown is reputed to have said of the Architecture School at UCLA, 'It's a true Southern California building with five entrances, none of which is the main one'. This penetrability throws greater functional loading on the surrounding environment and its design – if any! In domestic work the planting and landscaping is apt to have to work hard in an environmental sense, whether it is screening the living areas from prying eyes or a tidal wave of freeway noise; in public buildings external circulation and its interfaces with internal circulation (or in plain English, the parking lots) become critical [21]; and in both cases these vital external designed areas can sometimes command a greater square-footage than what is nominally 'inside' the structure. Conscious design, what Kenneth Clark has called 'willed architecture', has sometimes been slow in acknowledging these requirements, or – rather – it seems often to have acknowledged them almost by inadvertence while pursuing some other Angeleno end such as throwing dignity out the window or tackling the impossible. And sometimes when these problems have been recognized, their true import has not – notably in early attempts to pack parked cars tidily on top of supermarkets, for instance.

Such criticisms notwithstanding, the early modern architecture of Los Angeles is too functionally apt, environmentally ingenious, and aesthetically original to have deserved its almost total neglect by the authoritative historians of the period. Its claim to the world's attention was established well before 1914, but the very remoteness of Southern California, which had made the flowering of uninhibited architectural inventiveness possible, also locked it away in such isolation that the claim could hardly be seen or heard. In the twenties, time-lags in the publication of California architecture in even US magazines could run to four or five years after completion.

Furthermore the belief that Southern California was a crude, provincial sort of place (a belief that still persists in some quarters) has made it difficult, particularly for some European historians, to believe that these flowerings of originality were anything but derivative or shamelessly imitative (for instance, the attempts to show that Schindler must have seen European magazines and books in the early twenties). As a result there has been a general tendency to see Irving Gill as an inexplicable footnote to Adolf Loos, or the Greene Brothers as some kind of rustic cousins of the Wright clan – even

21. Dodger Stadium parking, Elysian Park, 1959

though Frank Lloyd Wright was not working in California until after the Greenes' best work was done.

Whatever historians have liked to believe, however, it remains difficult to understand how they could have failed to concede Los Angeles' comparable rank with Paris, Berlin, and Chicago in the history of domestic architecture in the present century; the quality and quantity of first-rate modern houses in the Los Angeles area is impressive by anybody's standards, and the fact that they are located in a city that departs from all the rules for 'civilized living' as they have been understood by the pundits of modernity makes their impact all the more powerful on the visitor.

Another confusing aspect of their impact is this: not only does this excellent domestic architecture *not* enjoy the kind of cultural support and background of building tradition that have been thought essential to modern architecture, but visibly it *does* enjoy the support of an influence and a tradition that would normally be thought positively harmful – the Spanish Colonial Revival. This is not easy to see at first because Spanish Colonial Revival is as protean in its variability as it is pervasive in its distribution; its presence is ultimately as easy to sense as its characteristics are initially difficult to define. As represented in a scholarly study like David Gebhard's article of 1967, it has to cover everything from the starkly geometric to the most wedding-cake fanciful, from the relaxedly folksy to the tautly professional. Such vagueness in the term's historical 'profile' is inevitable in the loose way that it has been used to cover all kinds of romantic fancy-dress architecture from imitation adobes to full-fledged and erudite revivals of the Churrigueresque, but no useful service would be performed by attempting to render the term Spanish Colonial Revival any more precise. Left vague, it serves conveniently to cover a variety of building of generically Hispanic inspiration that has become almost the most natural way of building anywhere in Southern California; any building design that actively engages with the ecological and psychological facts of life in the area has a tendency to emerge with a Spanish Colonial Revival air of some sort, even though there is no single detail or usage at which the historian can point to identify the style.

So, for the purpose of the present study, Spanish Colonial Revival will not be treated as an identifiable or consciously adopted style, but as something which is ever-present and can be taken for granted, like the weather – worth comment when it is outstandingly beautiful or conspicuously horrible, but otherwise simply part of the day-to-day climate from which, as Gebhard rightly claims, much of modern California architecture derives.

The derivation becomes clear enough in the work of Irving Gill. It is what distinguishes his architecture from that of Adolf Loos, with whom he is persistently compared; whereas the white bald surfaces and forms of Loos are so often merely negative protestations of revolt and disgust, those of Gill are quietly affirmative; a positive morality, not a subtractive one. The Hispanic element is also what separates Gill's mature work from his prentice pieces. In those early works Gill – only two years younger than Frank Lloyd Wright and with even less formal training, though he had passed through Sullivan's office – is clearly a late exponent of the Shingle Style; the 'Mission' elements he is supposed to have taken east for his Rhode Island work of 1902 are much less notable than the Shingle (and even Prairie School) qualities he brought to his first California buildings. Nevertheless, by the time he came to build his first house in Los Angeles proper, the Laughlin residence [22] on 28th Street, in 1907, he already commanded much of his newly discovered Hispanic repertoire: the flat white-stuccoed walls, the tiled roof, the round-topped openings on the ground floor and the bracketed balconies on the floor above. Such a catalogue sounds like the mannerisms of an avowed Spanish Colonial Revivalist such as George Washington Smith in Santa Barbara, but the Herberton house, the first work of Smith in the manner, was a decade later. More to the point, what are romantic mannerisms, skilfully deployed, in the work of

Smith, represent something deeper and more unified and quietly tough-minded in the work of Gill.

The true mark of this deeper and more unified discipline in Gill's work is his progressive ability to dispense with architectural detailing in the conventional or pattern-book sense. It survives, minimally, in the Laughlin house, but the true meaning of the Hispanic tradition for

22. Laughlin house, 28th Street, 1907, Irving Gill, architect

23. Dodge house, King's Road, 1916 (demolished), Irving Gill, architect

Gill was as a guide towards a simplified clean-edged architecture, something like that which was beginning to attract his European contemporaries and their followers. His difference from them lies in his lack of mechanistic pretensions, and also that lack of ferocious introspection that gives European work of the twenties that air of *angst* which has become its guarantee of probity in the eyes of later generations. The use of skinny metal mullions and frames in Gill's windows, like the advanced tilt-slab technique for pouring concrete walls, never seems to imply a desire to prove a point about the Machine Age, never prevents him using classical columns to support the woodwork of a pergola, for instance. The flat white single-storey façade of his railroad station in Torrance is pierced by a wide rect-angular entrance framing four unfluted Doric columns *in antis* – and in 1913, when no European modernist could have done it without embarrassment, such unobtrusive self-confidence is slyly exhilarating.

Irving Gill's great contribution to Los Angeles, and perhaps his best building ever, was the Dodge house in King's Road, finished in 1916 [23]. After protracted years of uncertainty its demolition has been greeted with expressions of popular outrage – of all works of 'fine' architecture in the area it had qualities most immediately accessible to lay understandings. (I myself encountered two gentle hippies in its garden who inquired, with great formality, who was 'the owner of this beautiful residence', and were stunned to hear that it might be pulled down to make way for an apartment development.) Even its sheer size was impressive, but it was not bulk alone that gave it such an air of easy monumentality; it was the relation of the plain white-wall surfaces to the square window-openings and to the round-headed doors, arcades, and *porte-cochère* at ground-floor level.

Internally this broad simplicity of surface was even more striking; walls around the staircase in the entrance hall were panelled flush in uninterrupted planes of Honduras mahogany, into which the plain square sticks of the balustrade, and flat fronts of the drawers of the storage wall, were simply recessed. Though much comment on the modernity of the house has concentrated, and rightly, on its mechanical ingenuities (such as the central vacuum-cleaning system with hose outlets in the skirtings) this extensive wooden structure throughout the hall area was even more striking to me. Its succession of flat rectangular planes in space seems to be one of those very rare links between the otherwise unconnected periods of modern architecture in Los Angeles, anticipating the kind of interior design that is found in some early works of Neutra.

How consequential a link might be is difficult to say; the Dodge house was almost the last major work that Gill was to do in Los Angeles, thirteen years before Neutra's Lovell house, though there was to be one other work of intriguing quality – the delicious Horatio West apartments [24] in Santa Monica of 1919. Like the earlier Lewis Courts in Sierra Madre, this is a patio scheme, but unlike the broad central court at Sierra Madre, the internal space at San Mo, broken

24. Horatio West apartments, Santa Monica, 1919

into by arcades on either side, is so narrow that one could easily mistake it for an automobile drive-way. In any case, the great feature of the design is its upstairs living rooms, glazed around three sides to command views of sea and mountains that must have been well worth the rental when it was first built. The whole conception takes Gill a long way beyond his Hispanic inspirations and a long way towards full modernism (if the term meant anything to him) of the sort that was to appear later in the work of Gropius and Le Corbusier.

25. Millard house, Pasadena, 1923, Frank Lloyd Wright, architect

Comparisons of this sort between California and Europe can be instructive to the point of being unsettling; Gill, after all, was of the generation of Lutyens, who never crossed the generation gap to modern architecture, and of Loos and Mackintosh who came up to the gap but never crossed it, and of Wright, whom Southern California provided with building opportunities when hardly anybody else wished to know him outside Japan – five major commissions in Los Angeles between 1917 and 1923 did much to fill what might otherwise have

26. Ennis house, Griffith Park, 1924, Frank Lloyd Wright, architect

been a very barren period of his life. As a consequence, Griffith Park, Pasadena, and the Hollywood Hills offer some of his most powerful and disturbing designs; the permissive free-swinging cultural style of Los Angeles gave his thwarted talents a chance to design works as seductive as La Miniatura [25], or as rhetorical as the Ennis house [26], crouching on its ridge and keeping watch and ward over the city spread below.

The brothers Greene were of this generation too, and fit better into the common expectations of the architecture of the time – at least at first sight. They had a good conventional training involving MIT and the influence of H. H. Richardson as transmitted to Henry Greene via the office traditions of Shepley, Rutan, and Coolidge in Boston, and their full unconventionality was a long time emerging. But when it did emerge, it came full flood and in a short period of years,

27. Blacker house, Pasadena, 1906, Greene and Greene, architects

and is seen at its best in their Pasadena houses, ten of which – including
the two masterworks for the Blacker [27] and Gamble families – were
done between 1905 and 1909. As late as the Culbertson house of 1902
they were working in a sub-Shingle style comparable to Gill's in that
year, but then they headed in the opposite direction entirely, plunging
into the complexities and potentialities of wooden construction as a
medium for architectural expression liberated beyond anything in the
East or the Middle West (whatever their debts to sources in those
parts). Common historical convention tends to attribute the liberated
style and other peculiarities of these houses to Japanese influences, but
this is an oversimplification that will not stand up on closer acquaintance.

My own closer acquaintance is with the Gamble house [28a, b] of
1908, which I inhabited from time to time, and the first thing that
residential familiarity taught me was that the fundamental quality of

28a. Gamble house, Pasadena, 1908, Greene and Greene, architects

28b. Gamble house, Pasadena, 1908, Greene and Greene, architects

these houses is sheer space. Admittedly the Gamble house is pretty big for a winter cottage even of that affluent period – some 8,000 square feet of indoor floor-space, and another 2,000 of covered terraces and sleeping porches. But it is more than the quantity of space that registers, it is the easy open-handed and informal way in which the individual spaces fit together, and how very formal some of these informally grouped spaces can be – the dining-room and the big living-room on the ground floor both have strict biaxial symmetry in plan, and the master bedroom upstairs is planned as a clear square with two rectangular sub-spaces, one providing a kind of entrance lobby and access to a giant wardrobe, the other creating a kind of inglenook around the fireplace, whence a curiously artistic (or possibly Moorish) little bay window looks back into the staircase.

But tangled all through this play of wide domestic spaces, uniting and differentiating them, is the Greenes' obsession with wooden construction and with visible craftsmanship. This obsession neatly footnotes Gebhard's observation of the way that European art-movements – in this case Arts and Crafts – lose their moral content and become forms of styling when they arrive on US soil. If the Gamble house is one of the ultimate gems of the Craftsman Movement in California it is also – in part – a paste jewel. Look into the roof spaces and you will find that the construction of what isn't seen, far from being carefully and lovingly wrought, tends to be the usual old US carpenter's crudwork, trued up with odd ends of lumber and spiked together with cock-eyed six-inch nails.

But everything that is meant to be seen has been wrought with care and artistry beyond belief, every piece of timber having been shaped, finished and polished, and exposed ends snubbed off with subtly curved edges. It is totally unlike any Japanese traditional domestic construction, such as we know from the Katsura detached palace; rather, the chosen vocabulary of shapes seems to derive from *netsuke* carving (in other houses pieces of jade from the family collections were incorporated in lampshades) and even more from the conventions for clouds and mist that one sees in *ukiyo-ye* prints and which are occasionally reproduced in the applied art work (carved panels in overmantels in the Culbertson house, for instance) of the Greenes' other houses.

In any case, these details do not form part of a general system of construction that bears much resemblance to anything oriental. Direct confrontation with the physical facts of the house is more likely to remind visitors of European wooden architecture of a sophisticated peasant type – Alpine in the forms of the roofs and exterior porches, Scandinavian in much of the visible structure, or even Russian, particularly in the splendid but rarely illustrated play-room in the upper part of the roof, with its low exposed trusses and its pannelled walls. In other words, and irrespective of the background and training of the architects, what they and their craftsmen were really assembling here was a poetic and romantic summary of the kind of wood-building traditions that Europeans had brought to the US from their home lands and had then diversified and refined on the long trek West. The Gamble house is a great romantic house, perhaps the finest in the world – because it is another monument to an American dream that was consummated in Southern California, and is as true a testimonial to what Los Angeles is all about as that other dream-monument, Simon Rodia's Towers in Watts.

But unlike the Towers it is not inimitable; the offspring of the Greenes' Pasadena houses are legion because they provided basic concepts and usages for the local manifestations of the California Bungalow tradition. In Pasadena itself, in Santa Monica, in the hills above Echo Park [29], anywhere at all that was developed in the teens and twenties of this century, you will find the open-truss porches, low spreading roofs, shingles and exposed rafter ends of this tradition alongside the stucco and arches of the Spanish Colonial Revival.

Thus the works of Southern California's pioneers of modern architecture, Irving Gill and Charles and Henry Greene, probably

29. California bungalows, Echo Park, *c.* 1920

gave less directly to the continuing but tenuous traditions of modern architecture than they did to the two local vernaculars from which modern architecture draws and to which modern architecture contributes. One is the Hispanic mode, the other, still without a convincing label beyond 'California Bungalow' (which no longer fits it adequately) is the generalized idiom (like the Shingle Style in the rest of the U S) of low pitched oversailing roofs and wooden walls, open fireplaces and rough timber, that belongs so much to the restaurant trade in Southern California that it could carry the soubriquet 'Gourmet Ranch-house Style'.

4　The Transportation Palimpsest

'A city built on transport' – like all truisms it offers a misleading truth, because it is persistently interpreted as referring only to automobile transport, and that interpretation is so trivial and so shallow historically that its use casts doubts on the right of the user to speak. Motorized transportation is almost as much of a recent epiphenomenon on the basic city of Los Angeles as it is in any other major metropolis. However, the less densely built-up urban structure of the Los Angeles basin has permitted more conspicuous adaptations to be made for motor transport than would be possible elsewhere without wrecking the city.

The fact that these parking-lots, freeways, drive-ins, and other facilities have not wrecked the city-form is due chiefly to the fact that Los Angeles has no urban form at all in the commonly accepted sense. But the automobile is not responsible for that situation, however much it may profit by it. The uniquely even, thin and homogeneous spread of development that has been able to absorb the monuments of the freeway system without serious strain (so far, at least) owes its origins to earlier modes of transportation and the patterns of land development that went with them. The freeway system is the third or fourth transportation diagram drawn on a map that is a deep palimpsest of earlier methods of moving about the basin.

In the beginning was the Camino Real, the Spaniards' military road (if anything so tenuous deserves so positive a name) with its military bases, missions, and *assistencias*, wandering with seasonal variations across the present Los Angeles area from south-east to north-west on its way to the northern presidios of Monterey and San Francisco. Its exact route seems pretty difficult to establish nowadays, though it is widely held to have followed something like the line of the present Wilshire Boulevard from the pueblo to the La Brea tar-pits (that is, from present downtown to Hancock Park) and then turned north over the Cahuenga pass into the San Fernando Valley. By the time the Yankees moved in, or very soon after, there must have been a well-established track running down to San Pedro, along which the ox-drawn carretas could rumble on their massive wheels, and by the end of the sixties there began to be a well-beaten track branching off the Camino Real to go down to Santa Monica, and so forth. But movement was painfully slow; two days to Santa Monica, and in the memories of the grandparents of men my own age it could take up to a week to get into the downtown area from the farms south of Riverside with a loaded wagon.

While transportation remained in this condition, the pueblo city of Los Angeles could not hope to be more than a minor market-town – so things could not be allowed to remain in that condition for long after the ambitious Yankees arrived, and on this point there was sufficient consensus for community action. However much the pioneer railroad [30] down to the harbour at San Pedro may have served the private ends of its chief promoter, Phineas Banning, owner of the rancho-land where the new port would be built, the railway was financed with public money – bond-issues by the City of Los Angeles and the County. The line began operation in 1869, connecting the business community in the city with deep-water anchorages at Wilmington / San Pedro, where, after Banning's dredging activities, there was eighteen feet draught clearance over the sand-bar.

Yet it now appears that the true importance of the Wilmington line was less in its inherent usefulness than as a negotiable property or bargaining-counter in the railroad deals of the next decade. When that same business community discovered that the Southern Pacific line from San Francisco to Yuma might ignore them and go straight across the high desert, they could see only economic stagnation in a future that would leave them disconnected from direct access to the trans-continental railroads – few cities bypassed by the main trunk routes prospered. So they had to bestir themselves again and the infant

Wilmington line was part of the king's ransom the Southern Pacific extracted from Los Angeles before they would agree to divert their line south over the Soledad pass, and down through the San Fernando Valley into the pueblo and then east to San Bernardino and on to Yuma.

This arrangement was patently useful to the SP, who could bring heavy equipment and materials ashore at Wilmington and up the city's line, and then build out east and west from the pueblo, instead of having to overland everything through the San Joaquin Valley from San Francisco. The conclusion of the deal was also, as far as anyone can judge, the most important single event in the history of the area after the foundation of the pueblo in 1781, and considerably more consequential than anything since.

The terms of the deal with the SP began to shape the future super-city almost at once. Construction began in three directions from the pueblo: north to San Fernando, east to Spadra en route to San Bernardino, both as part of the transcontinental linkage, and south-east to the vineyard colony at Anaheim – a *quid pro quo* for the County. The first train ran from San Fernando to Spadra in 1874, and in the same year Senator J. P. Jones of Nevada floated a rival company to build a line from the pueblo to deep water at Santa Monica, to be connected back inland with the SP's competitors, the Union Pacific. In the upshot it was to be a decade before any transcontinental line beside the SP came over the mountains into Los Angeles, but Jones's thwarted plan gave Los Angeles the Santa Monica line.

These five lines radiating from the pueblo towards San Fernando, San Bernardino, Anaheim, Wilmington, and Santa Monica constitute the bones of the skeleton on which Greater Los Angeles was to be built, the fundamentals of the present city where each of these old lines is now duplicated by a freeway – on the San Bernardino freeway, tracks run down the central reservation for some miles, so close is the agreement between the rail and road networks. But these lines did more than provide the skeleton, they brought the flesh. Subdivision of adjoining land proceeded as fast as the laying of rails – construction of the Santa Monica line began in January 1875, and land sales began in Santa Monica itself in July the same year. More important, if the words of J. J. Warner in 1876 mean what they appear to mean, then commuting began almost as soon as the rails were down – 'Daily we go to breakfast in Los Angeles from San Bernardino, and back to its fountains and groves 'ere nightfall'. Before 1880 then, the railways had outlined the form of the city and sketched in the pattern of movement that was to characterize its peculiar style of life.

Shortly after 1880, too, the railroads were to bring in the Angelenos in something like their present quantities. Once the Santa Fé had come down the Cajon pass into San Bernardino from the desert, and then west to the pueblo in 1885, there were two genuinely competitive transcontinental systems serving the area, and in the ensuing rate-war, fares from Kansas City were at one point cut to one dollar – 'one single silver dollar'. The first great wave of immigration from the Middle West poured into Southern California and precipitated a land boom that lasted almost a decade. And although paper fortunes were made and lost with the usual legendary rapidity and parcels of land changed hands several times a day and all the rest of it, the final collapse of the boom seems to have been far less disastrous than in the normal scenario for such affairs; land-speculation remains a major industry still. Yet, with a rising tide of human immigration coming in, and the process of land-subdivision proceeding with the usual US enthusiasm, why was the result not the usual outward sprawl from a central nucleus? The pueblo/downtown area did indeed concentrate the bulk of the population in the second half of the last century, but the nearer to the end of the century the less convincing its dominance – the immigrants who came in after 1885 tended to broadcast themselves more evenly across the face of the land.

In this trend a number of factors were involved. First, a very large proportion of the immigrant population came from thinly peopled farming areas in the Middle West and their intention in California was to farm – they had the habits and the intentions of a dispersed way of living. They could settle anywhere that was served by water and transportation – and the transportation was there even before they arrived. Furthermore, the railway promoters worked closely with the subdividers, creating town-sites along the tracks. Some of these speculations faded away again, leaving only a pattern of pegs in the ground, marking the unbought lots. Others took root however, and formed centres of settlement and development with an economic and municipal life somewhat independent of downtown. But the speculators could not develop land that was not theirs to subdivide; the order in which the rancho lands were sold off by the grant holders and their successors was another dispersive factor; Santa Monica may have been subdivided in 1875, but adjoining San José de Buenos Aires just inland was not successfully subdivided until half a century later.

But the greatest dispersive factor is what is hinted at in Warner's apparent reference to commuting habits; given a railway system it was as convenient to live in San Bernardino or Santa Monica as on the outer fringes of the central city, especially where those fringes were ill served by any form of transportation, as they were until after the railway age had begun. Judge Widney's Spring and Sixth Street line opened operations with its horse-drawn street-cars only in 1874, to connect the then business area with the fashionable residential zone around Spring and Hill, and in the next fifteen years other street-car lines opened in Pasadena, Pomona, Santa Monica, San Bernardino and Ontario (where the mules rode back down the long gentle slope of Euclid Avenue on special flat-trucks behind the cars, which were powered by gravity in this direction). But by that time – by 1887 in fact – George Howland's Pico Street line was operating out of downtown to serve the 'Electric Railway Homestead Association Tract' and the definitive age of the development of Los Angeles had begun.

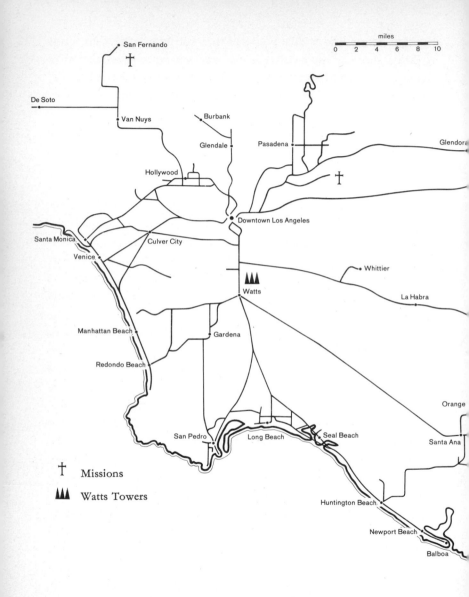

miles
0 2 4 6 8 10

San Fernando

De Soto

Van Nuys

Burbank

Glendale

Pasadena

Glendora

Hollywood

Downtown Los Angeles

Santa Monica

Culver City

Venice

Whittier

Watts

La Habra

Manhattan Beach

Gardena

Redondo Beach

Orange

San Pedro

Long Beach

Seal Beach

Santa Ana

† Missions

▲▲▲ Watts Towers

Huntington Beach

Newport Beach

Balboa

30. Route map of the Pacific Electric Railway, 1923

Local electric services by street railways and inter-urban lines were to make almost every piece of land in the Los Angeles basin conveniently accessible and thus profitably exploitable, and the Pico line was the true beginning of the process, not only because it was

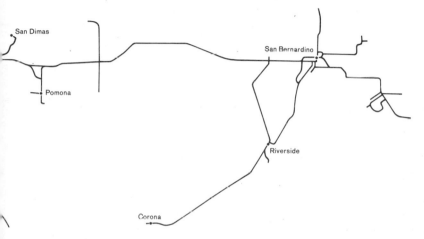

directly linked to a subdividing company, but because it also formed the basis of the early speculations of Sherman and Clark, pioneers of the get-rich-quick electric railway. They seem to have been primarily speculators ('General' Moses Sherman liked to have a finger in every profitable pie within reach) whose companies floated, grew, collapsed, merged, came and went, were wrested from them by outraged shareholders, but popped up again under different guises. In the process, lines were built down to the University of Southern California and up to Pasadena (largely by merging and connecting existing local companies) and, in 'Sherman's March to the Sea', out through Hollywood to Santa Monica with an extension to Ocean Park in 1896 – perhaps the most important of all their ventures since it provided the transportation infrastructure for an area of land that was to contribute much to the present character of the city.

But Sherman and Clark were small fry compared to the next generation of electric railway promoters, especially Henry Edmunds
Huntington, son of Collis P. Huntington of Southern Pacific fame. In
fifteen years of wheeling, dealing, buying-out the Santa Monica
network, beating off rivals (including, confusingly enough, the
Southern Pacific from time to time), consolidations and reorganizations,
culminating in the 'great merger' he gave the city the Pacific Electric
Railway (and, out of the proceeds, his palace in San Marino as the
Huntington Museum and Library). The PE's 'Big Red Cars', so called
to distinguish them from the narrow-gauge street railways operated by
the associated Los Angeles Railway Co., operated over standard-
gauge tracks that ran, for much of their lengths, over private rights-of-
way, avoiding the congestion of the streets, though they had to become
street railways when they entered already well-developed areas,
running in central or lateral reservations.

The Big Red Cars ran all over the Los Angeles area – literally all
over. The route map of the PE [30] at its point of greatest extension,
when it operated 1,164 miles of track in fifty-odd communities pretty
well defines Greater Los Angeles as it is today. Services ran down
the coast to Balboa and along the foot of the Palisades to the mouth of
Santa Monica Canyon; up into the valley and to San Fernando; to
Riverside, Corona, and San Bernardino; out through La Habra and
through Anaheim to Orange; through the foothill cities of the Sierra
Madre to Glendora, and via Pasadena to Echo Canyon and Mount
Lowe. Within the area laced by this network the stops and terminals
already bore the names of streets and localities that are current today.
Not only did the PE outline the present form of Los Angeles, it also
filled in much of its internal topography, since its activities were
everywhere involved – directly or otherwise – with real estate.

Yet real estate was to be one of the two factors that undid this
masterpiece of urban rapid transport. As subdivision and building

promoted profitably increased traffic, they also produced more inter-sections and grade crossings where trains could be held up and schedules disrupted, so that the service began to deteriorate and street accidents began, in the twenties, to give the Big Red Cars a bad name. And what was obstructing the grade crossings and involved in helping to cause the street accidents was the other factor in the undoing of the PE; the automobile.

Convenient as the services of the PE might be, the door-to-door private car was even more convenient in this dispersed city, and had begun to proliferate in the area even before the inter-urban railway network reached its operational peak. As early as 1915 the automobile had begun to steal custom directly from the PE, since it was used for the Jitney services that cruised the main streets and avenues picking up waiting passengers at the trolley stops. Even so, it took the automobile an unconscionable time to kill off the PE (partly because of shortages and rationing in the Second World War) and it was not until 1961 that the last train ran on the line through Watts to Long Beach – both places virtual creations of the PE.

By that time the city had already embarked on a programme of studies in the kind of Urban Rapid Transit now fashionable in city-planning circles (e.g. San Francisco's BART line), but it looks like being a long time before anything serious is done about it. It will not be easy to persuade Angelenos, many of them able to remember the dying agonies of the PE, to leave the convenient car at home – in spite of their complaints about traffic jams – and climb into whatever coloured rolling-stock the new dream-system offers. As Ray Bradbury (a non-driving Angeleno) rightly said in 1960:

. . . it's no use building it unless we dramatize it enough to make people use it. I'm all for making Walt Disney our next Mayor . . . the only man in the city who can get a working rapid transit system built without any more surveys, and turn it into a real attraction so that people will want to ride it.

The city got Sam Yorty for its next Mayor and Walt Disney died and rapid transit is presumably postponed till the Greek Kalends. The automobile remains the characteristic transportation of Angelenos.

The date when it became characteristic is not easy to fix. The Automobile Club of Southern California has been incapable of conceiving any other form of movement ever since its foundation in 1900, but is notoriously among the most bigoted lobbies operating in the area (which is quite an achievement in that stronghold of the John Birch Society). But if one takes the conscious provision of large-scale specialized facilities for automobiles as marking their effective ascendancy, then the establishment of the Motor Age in Los Angeles dates neither from the foundation of the Automobile Club, nor from the building of the first freeway, but from about 1927.

Now, one of the attractions of the automobile in a dispersed and relatively under-equipped community is that it requires, fundamentally, very few special facilities – it will run tolerably on any fairly flat, hard surface. So Sunset Boulevard was not surfaced at all beyond Fairfax Avenue as late as 1927. But in that year work was already in hand on the first real monument of the Motor Age: Miracle Mile on Wilshire Boulevard. The Boulevard itself was the creation of years of *ad hoc* subdivisions, beginning with a quarter-mile stretch west of the present McArthur Park laid out in 1895 by the ineffable Gaylord Wilshire – socialist, enthusiast, medical crank but – more to the point – member of a clan that had already developed parts of Fullerton and knew their business. Further west, the stretch of the Boulevard through Beverly Hills was regularized as part of Wilbur Cook's plan of 1906, and the continuation to the sea at Santa Monica was completed in 1919. But the eastward extension into downtown, which converted West Lake Park into McArthur Park as we know it, was not made until 1934 – after some dogged resistance from downtown interests to whom the shops on Wilshire constituted a grave commercial threat. The possibilities of shopping on Wilshire had been spotted about a decade before, by

A. W. Ross, a real estate operator who had looked into the probable shopping habits of the new, affluent, and motorized inhabitants of areas like Beverly Hills, the westerly parts of Hollywood, or the areas of the Wolfskill Ranch that were about to become Westwood and Holmby Hills. The chances appeared to be that they would prefer to come to shops along the stretch of Wilshire between La Brea and Fairfax, and by 1928 this stretch was already known as Miracle Mile.

But it was not open to unlimited commercial development. Downtown interests had wanted it to be a broad residential avenue, not a

31. Parking behind Wilshire Boulevard

32. Arroyo Seco Parkway, 1939

business rival, and the city had zoned it accordingly. Ross therefore had to negotiate or litigate a 'spot' waiver to the residential zoning for every site, and this he could only do for substantial and well-regarded clients who would not lower the supposed tone of the street. But substantial operators were in the mood to move, and the mighty Bullock's department store was ready for Wilshire Boulevard by 1928, though their chosen site was further east, not on Miracle Mile proper. But Bullock's-Wilshire, like the new shops on the mile, were all built with parking-lots at the rear [31] and were specifically designed for motorized access, with *portes-cochères* or other specialized entrance facilities on the parking side.

The result is a unique transitional monument to the dawn of auto-mobilism; the shops on Miracle Mile stand hard up to the sidewalk so that it looks like a conventional shopping street, except that it is not clogged with cars mis-parked in desperation by frustrated shoppers. All but a few of them are safely and correctly stowed away round the back, and Wilshire Boulevard is one of the few great streets in the world where driving is a pleasure. It is also, of course, the first linear downtown, with residential areas immediately behind the parking-lots and almost seventy thousand souls within walking distance, never mind the motorized shoppers from a city-wide catchment area.

More conventional public provisions for the automotive age began in the same years as Miracle Mile: the upgrading of nondescript through-streets to the status of Boulevards (though long stretches of Santa Monica and Pico, for instance, are still pretty nondescript for mile after mile), the installation of traffic signals (synchronized, for the first time, on Wilshire) and the Figueroa Street grade separation in the north-east corner of downtown. This last – a simple enough underpass in its origins – is another historical landmark of importance, since it was the first of the works that eventually led to the Arroyo Seco Parkway, otherwise the Pasadena Freeway, the beginning of the freeway network.

The grade separation was begun early in 1938, the Automobile Club's celebrated Traffic Survey proposing a freeway system had been published the previous year, and the State of California legislation that made the freeways possible followed in 1939, by which time the Arroyo Seco Parkway was well in hand. It was only six miles long, and it was a parkway for a variety of reasons. One was emulation of Robert Moses's celebrated parkway system in New York; another was to mollify local opinion, since the side had been sliced off Elysian Park and the park strip in the bottom of the Arroyo had been extensively invaded by the time the highway reached Raymond Hill and curled round into Pasadena. No doubt *Sunset* magazine, the official organ of obsessive gardening and planting in Southern California, had a hand in the parkway concept too. Certainly the magazine is credited with a lobby that has sustained the parkway tradition ever since, so that – however much one may be amused at the signs on the freeways warning *Danger Landscaping Ahead* – one can still be grateful for this sustained programme of planting and improvement that has made the freeway embankments and cuttings a visible environmental asset to the city (even if freeway noise and dirt are not).

The Arroyo Seco Parkway [32] was the only section of the freeway system completed before the Second World War. The first of the post-war links, the Hollywood, went over the mountain into the San Fernando Valley, its southward extension became the Santa Ana (of ill repute, because of its jams and accidents) and the Pasadena's southern leg became the Harbor Freeway. This may sound like rapid progress, but freeway building has not been as fast as is sometimes supposed – the San Diego was not over the Santa Monica mountains into the valley until 1962, and my first road map of Los Angeles, printed in 1964, still did not show the western end of the Santa Monica freeway.

Thus the wide-swinging curved ramps of the intersection of the Santa Monica and the San Diego freeways, which immediately persuaded me that the Los Angeles freeway system is indeed one of the greater works of Man, must be among the younger monuments of the system. It is more customary to praise the famous four-level intersection which now looks down on the old Figueroa Street grade separation, but its virtues seem to me little more than statistical whereas the Santa Monica / San Diego intersection [33] is a work of art,

33a. Intersection of Santa Monica and San Diego freeways

33b. Intersection of Santa Monica and San Diego freeways

both as a pattern on the map, as a monument against the sky, and as a kinetic experience as one sweeps through it.

And what comes next? The freeway system is not perfect – what transport system ever is? – and even though it is vastly better than any other urban motorway system of my acquaintance, it is inconceivable to Angelenos that it should not be replaced by an even better system nearer to the perfection they are always seeking. A rapid-rail system is the oldest candidate for the succession, but nothing has happened so far. The core of the problem, I suspect, is that when the socially necessary branch has been built, to Watts, and the profitable branch, along Wilshire, little more will be done and most Angelenos will be an average of fifteen miles from a rapid-transit station.

The next candidate was the Superfreeway, with access only from existing freeways, not from surface streets. This one never seems to have got beyond the status of a cocktail-party topic – better performance can probably be got by filling out more of the proposed grid of the present freeway system [34] to increase the number of usable alternative routes. As currently proposed, the grid would give 1,500 miles of freeways on a pattern of approximate three-mile squares. After the Superfreeway came the urban helicopter, connecting landing pads next to freeway intersections and served by freeway-flyer bus services (which had been proposed independently as the simplest way of putting Watts back in touch with the city).

And then in 1969 it was suddenly observed that the fifth diagram of the transportation palimpsest had been drawn, not in fancy but in fact. It was in the air above the Angeleno's heads, but it was not the helicopters that planners and professional visionaries had led them to expect. With hindsight, one can now see that in a city as dis-urban as Los Angeles, the answer was more likely to be rural than conventionally urban, and what the Angelenos could see over their heads was usually that most rural of aircraft, the Twin Otter, designed for bushwhacking the outbacks of Canada. As an urban commuter plane it has the prime rural virtue of short take-off and landing runs (STOL) which enable it to operate out of odd corners of larger airports or from small private and municipal airfields, much more cheaply than any helicopter, and to potter about in the clear airspace below the crowded jetways above.

Flying these bushcraft, airlines like Cable and Aero-Commuter are – at this writing – already offering a dozen daily scheduled flights between Los Angeles International Airport and all stops to Fullerton, Burbank, or El Monte, and twice that number of services to the alternative international airport at Ontario. In other words, the urban air-bus exists and is in regular service in Los Angeles. As with Miracle Mile, Los Angeles has done what we are always told it will do, but rarely does in fact – prototyped a new solution for other cities to contemplate.

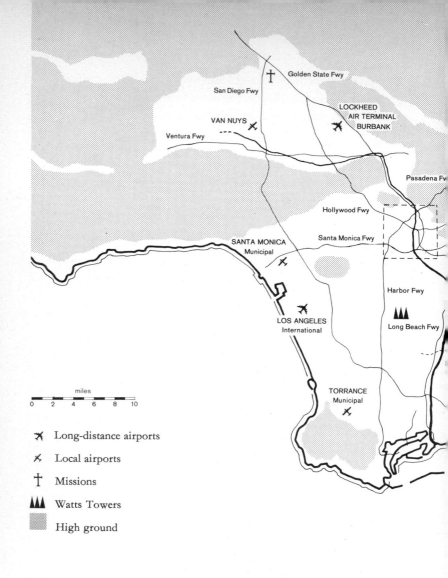

Golden State Fwy

San Diego Fwy

LOCKHEED
AIR TERMINAL
BURBANK

VAN NUYS

Ventura Fwy

Pasadena Fw

Hollywood Fwy

SANTA MONICA
Municipal

Santa Monica Fwy

Harbor Fwy

Long Beach Fwy

LOS ANGELES
International

miles

0   2   4   6   8   10

✈ Long-distance airports

✗ Local airports

† Missions

▲▲▲ Watts Towers

High ground

TORRANCE
Municipal

34. Map of Los Angeles freeways and airports

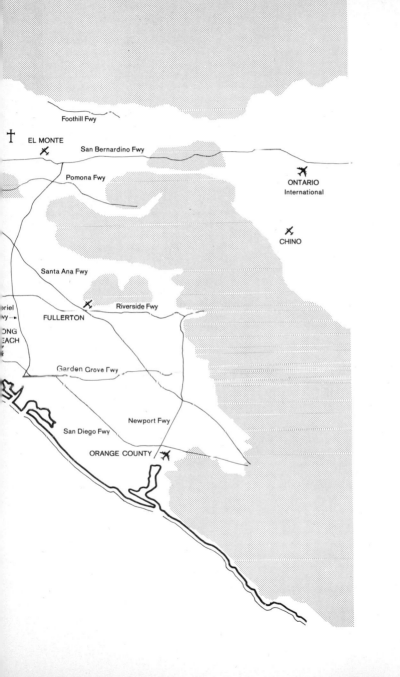

Foothill Fwy

EL MONTE

San Bernardino Fwy

ONTARIO
International

Pomona Fwy

CHINO

Santa Ana Fwy

riel
vy →

FULLERTON

Riverside Fwy

ONG
EACH

Garden Grove Fwy

Newport Fwy

San Diego Fwy

ORANGE COUNTY

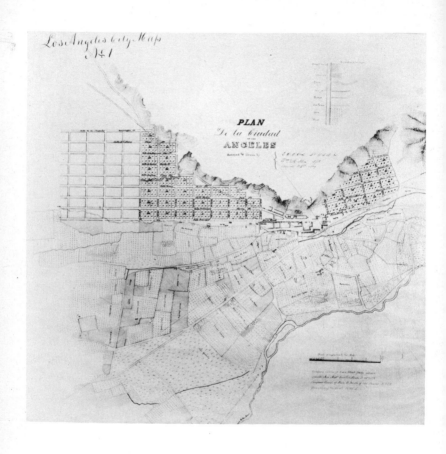

35. Survey of the pueblo by Lieutenant Ord, 1849

5 Ecology II: Foothills

Though the original pueblo of Los Angeles was built in the bottom-lands of the river valley, the site selected by Governor Felipe de Neve in 1781 is at the last point where the valley narrows, before the Los Angeles River loses itself southward into the plains on the way to the sea. Thus the original settlement could most easily be expanded approximately north and south along the river and did so, as the earliest US surveys of the town show, particularly in the creation of the first Mexican 'ghetto' – Sonora Town – to the north. But the customary type of US urban expansion, block by square block in all directions, would obviously engage the grid of streets with the adjoining hill-lands. The extensions proposed in Lieutenant Ord's survey of 1849 [35] sensibly stay on the flattish valley-bottom, but civilians cannot be relied on to go where the military direct them and the city was soon engaged with the small hills to east and west, and was building on their tops by the 1880s.

The characteristic townscape created in the process has almost entirely vanished – though the steeply-terraced rooming houses on either side of the Angel's Flight funicular railway [36] will be lovingly recalled by all fanciers of old private-detective movies. But that old high density development of the hillsides belonged to a primarily pedestrian concept of cities and their workings; they were but a tiny – if likeable – segment within a city whose conception of itself was neither figuratively nor physically pedestrian. All that Bunker Hill and the steeper parts of Boyle Heights had in common with the Los Angeles we know were the problems of footings and foundations on steep slopes made of little more than compacted sand.

By the middle seventies an alternative kind of hill country was being brought within sight of development – a kind of development that was to become highly typical of the area and pretty well unlike

36. Angel's Flight funicular railway, 1901 (demolished)

anything else in the world. Although the Santa Monica railway line was careful to run economically across the flat lands on its way to the sea, it had the lower slopes of the Hollywood Hills and the Santa Monica mountain handily to its north for almost its entire length, and it is upon that mountain that the classic Los Angeles foothill settlements were to appear.

Already in the eighties attempts were made to create cities between the mountain and the railroad. On the Wolfskill Ranch, in the tumbled lands where the present Wilshire Boulevard begins to turn south after

Beverly Glen, was founded the city of Sunset – from that point of vantage it might just have been possible to see the sun setting over the ocean beyond Santa Monica. In 1880 the inevitable resort hotel was built and land pegged out – and nothing happened and not a trace of it has been seen since. Further east, about where Cañon Drive now runs, another city, called Morocco, was laid out in 1888, and again seems to have vanished without trace. The full development of even these eminently desirable lands would have to wait, like so many other things in Los Angeles, for the electric trains, and these arrived with the Pasadena and Pacific lines of Sherman and Clark in 1895.

The classic spread of residential foothills now runs, westward in geographical order but not sequence of development, from Silverlake (built around the reservoir of that name), through Los Feliz (for want of a better name), Hollywood, West Hollywood, Beverly Hills, Bel Air, Brentwood, and Pacific Palisades where the foothills fall into the Pacific (literally so, after heavy rainstorms!). Eastward from the Los Angeles River, the sequence runs: Highland Park, Pasadena, San Marino to the south, Sierra Madre, and then they begin to tail off with decreasing conviction through Monrovia. This decrease of conviction stems from a basic socio-economic consideration which becomes stunningly apparent on any map that shows the distribution of average incomes; the financial and topographical contours correspond almost exactly: the higher the ground the higher the income. But – and this is where Los Angeles lines up with other cities for once – who ever heard of any rich suburbs much to the *east* of any downtown?

But south, of course, is a traditional area for superior suburbs in any city, and Los Angeles is no exception. The larger southerly enclave is on Palos Verdes mountain, whose inherently desirable landscape of broken grassland and planted woods with views over the sea contains the tremendously superior settlements of Palos Verdes, Palos Verdes Estates, Rolling Hills, and Rolling Hills Estates. The smaller southern enclave is an oddity; Baldwin Hills is an area of unlovely scrub largely given over to the oil industry, cross-country motor-cycling, or just waste, topped by a concrete reservoir that burst one memorable night in 1962 and is still dry. But on the north face (wrong, for a start; foothill settlements typically face south) and round to the east, is perfectly typical foothill development complete with tortuous roads and restrictive covenants in the title deeds which exclude Negroes and Mexicans. And at the foot of the slope is the rather untypical Baldwin Hills Village, a textbook example of a Radburn-planned super-block. Planning in any normal sense is not too common in Los Angeles (though there is more than might be expected) but its greatest example in the area is another foothill city, Beverly Hills.

As an example, Beverly Hills is almost too good; the regular pattern of lightly curving roads [37a, b] running north-west from Santa Monica

37a, b. Beverly Hills looking north in 1922, and in 1952

Boulevard, maintaining approximate symmetry about the double axis of Cañon and Beverly Drives, which cross when they intersect Sunset Boulevard, exchanging position in order to create the triangular site for the Beverly Hills Hotel ... that's all just drawing-board geometry, capable of absorbing the gentle rise in the land surface from Boulevard to Boulevard, but incapable of extension back into the broken country behind, where the pretty diagram begins to lose its symmetry and the streets rapidly abandon all pretence to geometrical order and become little more than black-topped mountain trails.

That is what the foothill ecology is really all about: narrow, tortuous residential roads serving precipitous house-plots that often back up directly on unimproved wilderness even now; an air of deeply buried privacy even in relatively broad valley-bottoms in Stone Canyon or

Mandeville Canyon. Even more than the second-growth woodlands of Connecticut or the heathlands of the Kentish Charts, this is landscape that seems to cry out for affluent suburban residences, and to flourish when so employed. Watered, it will carry almost any kind of vegetation that horticultural fantasy might conceive. Indeed, there is no native style of gardening in common practice at all, and cacti and other desert plants are quite difficult to find in the foothill cities. What are not difficult to find are laurels and other dense-growing small-leaved shrubs' that can be used to make thickets of instant privacy [38], essential to the fat life of the delectable mountains.

38. Townscape in Bel Air

The fat life is well known around the world, wherever television re-runs old movies on the Late Show or its local equivalent; it is the life, factual and fictional, of Hollywood's classic years. The outward show of this style is seen – with increasing difficulty through the occluding boscage – by the increasingly elderly patronage of the bus tours of Famous Film Stars' Homes; the inner workings of the style were as essential to the private detective movies as was the townscape of downtown – where would the private eyes of the forties have been without laurel shrubberies to lurk in, sweeping front drives to turn the car in, terraces from which to observe the garden below, massive Spanish Colonial Revival doors on which to knock, and tiled Spanish Colonial Revival interiors for the knocking to echo in, and the bars of Spanish Colonial Revival windows to hold on, or rambling split-level ranch house plans in which to lose the opposition, and random rubble fireplace walls to pin suspects against, and gigantic dream-bedrooms from which the sun may be seen rising in heart-breaking picture-postcard splendour over the Hollywood Hills . . . and the essential swimming pool for the bodies.

It was in this kind of residential landscape that the very real Bugsy Siegel was rubbed out; the world of the private eye was fact, and much of that fact survives. Visiting houses in Beverly Hills or Bel Air can be an hallucinating experience; an overwhelming sense of déjà vu mingles with an overwhelming desire to sidle along corridors with one's back to the wall and to kick doors wide open before passing through. The same urges seem not to be felt (by myself, at least) in the beach-houses of Malibu, however many movies they may have appeared in, which suggests that there is a peculiar authority about the Beverly Hills type of human ecology when seen and transmitted through the eyes of Hollywood – and so there should be; Hollywood Boulevard is the main street of the foothills [39], and Beverly Hills is where Hollywood lived from the time Douglas Fairbanks and Mary Pickford gave it the seal of approval by buying their piece of land on Summit Drive.

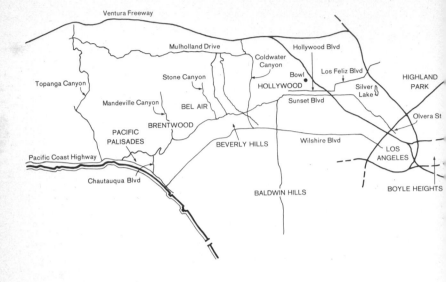

The sense of departed glory in those foothills is strong, but the built and planted structure remains almost untouched – this is still an immensely desirable human ecology for those who can afford it, and not just in Beverly Hills. The Rolls-Royces are still outside the door of the Blacker house in Pasadena and the Ferraris still negotiate the twisting roads of Palos Verdes as to the manner born, the Continentals turn in the forecourt of the Bel Air Hotel – and well-bred hooves still clatter in Mandeville Canyon. In so far as this ecology is threatened it is by its own desirability more than anything else; a desirability attested by the appearance of small two or three-storey apartment blocks balanced awkwardly over impossibly precipitous pocket handkerchief sites on the back lanes of Beverly Glen, and other areas beyond the zones developed by larger houses in the more accessible foothills.

They are one of the signs that this kind of domestic ecology is coming to an inevitable end. As back-lane development testifies, accessible and buildable sites are becoming more and more rare, and

39. Map of the foothill communities

few old ones have yet been liberated for redevelopment. More than this, steep foothill sites demand a building technology that is out of step with what is increasingly normal in Los Angeles today. Whether it is the crudest dingbat or something much more sophisticated, the Angeleno house of the sixties has tended to be the house of a plainsman, not a mountaineer. The economics of its structural technology imply a flat building-surface, not a sloping one; and those economics are demanding enough to ensure that the site will be a flat one by some means or other.

The common solution for a long time has been to create a framed substructure of some sort, with supporting posts and tiles and 'dead-men' to fix it back to the slope behind and stop the whole affair sliding. Craig Ellwood's Smith house [40] on Crestwood Drive is a classic of this kind of solution, because the flat-floored single-storeyed house is integrated with the supporting frame below, a common steel structure continuing the bay-system of his customary glass-box

40. Smith house, West Los Angeles, 1955, Craig Ellwood, architect

aesthetic down to the footings on the slope and leaving the space under-neath wide open. A more or less equivalent solution in wood, integrat-ing the sub-frame with the architecture above, can be seen in the Seidenbaum house off Mulholland Drive [41], designed by Richard Dorman, and much of the supposed eccentricity of the domestic architecture of John Lautner is traceable to the attempt to solve this kind of problem – his famous Chemosphere house [42] (also off Mul-holland) standing on its single concrete column is a very reasonable and well worked out solution, given the forty-five degree slope of the site. Alternatively, the un-thought-out solution – if solution it is – simply takes a standard developer's tract-house and perches it in mid-air on steel uprights, a surreal image of plainsmen's houses apparently airborne and detached from earth which can be seen to good (or ludicrous) effect on the San Fernando side of Coldwater Canyon, in Laurel Canyon, and elsewhere.

41. Seidenbaum house, Mulholland Drive, 1964, Richard Dorman, architect

42. Chemosphere house, Hollywood Hills, 1960, John Lautner, architect

43. Mountain cropping for house-building

However, the classic intrusions of plainsmen's housing into foot-hill ecology depend on a fundamentally different way of making the building surface flat – scraping away the mountain until you have enough horizontal surface, not to create merely a levelled terrace in front of a house but to create a street-sized terrace to carry a dozen or more houses, or a plateau big enough to carry a whole tract [43]. Given the basically sandy structure of the hills, and the sophistication of modern bulldozing, scraping, and grading equipment, mountains of this kind can be moved without much sweat, albeit plenty of noise and dust. Indeed, the greatest of all the monuments of the foothills is just such an earth-form (though basically a natural one), the Hollywood Bowl, home of the famous open-air concerts [44]. But 'mountain cropping' is not concerned with creating monuments of the earth-mover's art; just using earth-moving techniques to create an environ-ment where current tract-house building technology can operate by its

44. Hollywood Bowl, before alterations of 1969,
architectural design, Lloyd Wright

normal flatland habits. And this, apparently, is still the most economical
way of building in the foothills; architect-proposed alternatives, such as
cutting the price of sub-frames by mass-producing their component
parts seem to be non-starters for years a system of standardized sub-
frames covering a slope below Sunset Mesa stood abandoned with no
houses on it, and only a few have been built on it even now [45].

The effects of mountain-cropping techniques are obviously going to
be profound, ecologically and otherwise. Without joining the chorus of
doom from professional Jeremiahs at Berkeley and in the Sierra Club,
I must still admit that it proposes a different kind of ecological disturbance to those previously practised in Los Angeles. Though, obviously,
all building in foothill territory must involve some disturbance of the
soil, the customary methods of working and designing did not alter
the profiles of whole hills, exalt valleys, or make waste places plain, in
the way that large-scale mountain cropping does. Indeed, the whole-

45. House-frames, Sunset Mesa

sale planting probably helped to stabilize the land forms by thickening the root-mat and delaying water run-off. The existing and famous slide areas, which have provided literary minds with a ready-made metaphor of the alleged moral decay of Los Angeles, are usually associated with under-cutting rather than summit cropping – existing flat areas at the foot of sand cliffs have been cut into for road widening, or enlarging parking lots. This in itself may not increase the steepness of the slope beyond a seemingly safe angle of repose, but building, planting, etc. higher up the hill may have produced changes in drainage patterns sufficient to unsettle the whole bluff, and thus produce continuously crumbling cliffs like that above the Pacific Coast Highway at Chatauqua. This has produced at least one major fall a month whenever I have been staying in Los Angeles.

Whether the existing codes governing grading and filling work, which date only from 1952 in the city, and 1957 in the county, will be adequate for large-scale cropping remains to be seen – after the storms of 1969 I have my own doubts. Really big cropping like that at the top of Topanga Canyon involves cutting deep into the underlying geology, and totally filling ravines and other drainage runs, so it becomes difficult not to entertain apocalyptic queries about how some of these developments are going to settle down – and where! Such large-scale triflings with the none-too-stable structure of an area of high earthquake risk seems more portentous as a direct physical risk to life and limb than as a lost ecological amenity. Naturally one regrets the disappearance of Southern California's attractively half-tamed wildernesses, but short of a social revolution or major economic disaster they were going to get built on anyhow. The worry is that these extensive human settlements have been constructed on sands that have been shifted once by an outside agency, and may decide to shift for themselves at any time.

However, mountain cropping on this scale is currently restricted to the fringes of the Los Angeles area, and is nowhere yet on the cataclysmic scale of the reworked topographies further north – the most spectacular examples in *How to Kill a Golden State* by William Bronson (to whom I am indebted for the phrase 'mountain cropping') nearly all seem to be in San Mateo county, outside San Francisco and handily adjacent to the notorious San Andreas Fault. In the Los Angeles area the demand for hill-lands is not yet so acute; in the San Fernando Valley, in Orange County and on the fringes of the desert beyond the mountains there is land yet, accessible from the freeways, where the eternal plainsmen can settle and build for pleasure and, above all, for profit. While this persists, and the zoning ordinances are not too often waived, the original residential foothills can expect to remain mostly undisturbed, embosked ever deeper in their tortuous roads and laurel privacies, epitomes of the great middle-class suburban dream.

6 Architecture II: Fantastic

Like the film, the hamburger is a non-Californian invention that has achieved a kind of symbolic apotheosis in Los Angeles; symbolic, that is, of the way fantasy can lord it over function in Southern California. The purely functional hamburger, as delivered across the counter of say, the Gipsy Wagon on the UCLA campus, the Surf-boarder at Hermosa Beach or any McDonald's or Jack-in-the-Box outlet [46] anywhere, is a pretty well-balanced meal that he who runs (surfs, drives, studies) can eat with one hand; not only the ground beef but all the sauce, cheese, shredded lettuce, and other garnishes are firmly gripped between the two halves of the bun.

But the fantastic hamburger as served on a platter at a sit-down restaurant is something else again. Its component parts have been carefully opened up and separated out into an assemblage of functional and symbolic elements, or alternatively, a fantasia on functional themes. The two halves of the bun lie face up with the ground beef on one and, sometimes, the cheese on the other. Around and alongside on the platter are the lettuce leaves, gherkins, onion rings, fried potatoes, paper cups of relish or coleslaw, pineapple rings, and much more besides, because the invention of new varieties of hamburger is a major Angeleno culinary art. Assembled with proper care it can be a work of visual art as well; indeed, it must be considered as visual art first and foremost, since some components are present in too small a quantity generally to make a significant gustatory as opposed to visual contribution – for instance, the seemingly mandatory ring of red-dyed apple, which does a lot for the eye as a foil to the general greenery of the salads, but precious little for the palate.

The way in which the functional and symbolic parts of the hamburger platter have been discriminated, separated, and displayed is a fair analogue for the design of most of the buildings in which

they are sold. No nonsense about integrated design, every part conceived in separated isolation and made the most of; the architecture of symbolic assemblage. But it was not always so; the earlier architecture of commercial fantasy of the city tended to yield primacy to a single symbolic form or *Gestalt* into which everything had to be fitted. The famous Brown Derby restaurant in the shape of a hat [47], the Cream Cans (in the shape of cream cans), the Hoot Hoot I Scream outlet (in the form of an owl, not an ice-cream) and the several Bonzo dogs that sold hot dogs in the twenties and thirties, repackaged their functional propositions in symbolic envelopes expressing a single, formal idea.

The building and the symbol are one and the same thing, and if this sounds like one of the approved aims of architecture as a fine art, then it can certainly be paralleled in the work of reputable art architects of the period and later – Henry Oliver's Spadina house of

48. Grauman's Chinese Theatre, Hollywood, 1927,
Meyer and Holler, architects

1925, with its domestic functions re-packaged in a Hansel and Gretel
image, or almost any Angeleno building where a single idea has been
made dominant over everything else, most triumphantly, perhaps,
in Lloyd Wright's Wayfarer's Chapel of 1949 [15], which contrives to
command respect both as architecture in the respectable sense of the
word, and as Pop fantasy comparable to the wilder kind of gourmet-
style restaurants.

Such symbolic packaging within a single conceptual form can
impose strains even on a building with one function only to serve,
let alone a multiplicity of functions, and there were always needs that
drove fantasists in other directions. So Grauman's Chinese Theatre
[48], the ultimate shrine of all the fantasy that was Hollywood, kept
most of its fantastication as a garnish for the façade and the pavilions
flanking Meyer and Holler's generous forecourt, while the architecture

49. Richfield Building (demolished), downtown Los Angeles, 1928, Morgan Walls and Clements, architects

50 (*opposite*). Aztec Hotel, Monrovia, 1925, Robert Stacy-Judd, architect

underneath is plain bread-and-butter stuff like the buns of the hamburger. It is, indeed, a much less 'integrated design' than either of its two most celebrated fantastic contemporaries, both by Morgan Wall and Clements, the Assyrian-style Samson Rubber Company plant, and the recently demolished black-and-gold Richfield Building [49] downtown. But one other properly appliquéed fantasy does survive from the

twenties: the totally improbable Aztec Hotel in Monrovia [50]; intended by its designer to be Mayan rather than Aztec, it has his supposedly Mayan detailing stuck all over a relatively plain structure like piped icing on a pastry.

51. Bullock's-Wilshire, 1928,
Parkinson and Parkinson, architects

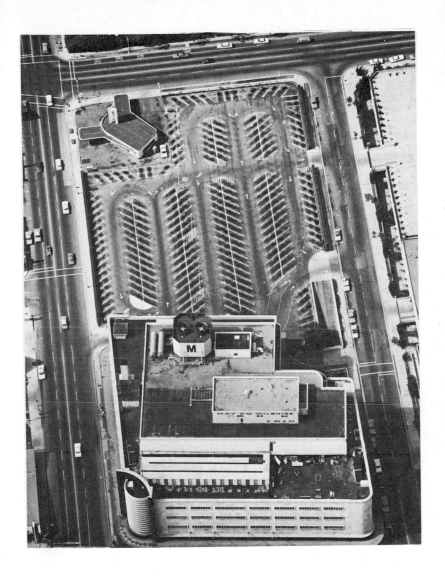

52. May Company, Miracle Mile, 1939,
Albert C. Martin and Associates, architects

Fantasy is actually found only rarely in the planning of a building, or the layout of adjoining clustered structures – even a much later fantasy such as the Bel Air hotel, laid out like a Spanish Colonial Revival village, finally proves to be a rational system of pedestrian courts – the real fantasy there is the 'outdoor' fireplace under a tree in a rockery at the end of the dining-room. Fantasy of the hamburger kind is all too often a compensation for the poverty of the building behind or under it, or for the hard-nosed rationalism of the market economy, and this division between the rational, functional shell and the fantastic garnish has become more apparent as the years have passed. On Wilshire Boulevard, and over a time-span of a decade, the development can be seen in the two prime department stores. Bullock's-Wilshire [51] has an eye-catching tower that grows naturally out of the detailing and structural rhythms of what is below, an immensely professional piece of architecture by Parkinson and Parkinson in 1929; May Company at the end of Miracle Mile has its equally eye-catching gilt cylinder chopped back into the corner of a rectangular shopping-box [52] to which it is related only by physical attachment, Albert C. Martin in 1939 having turned in a piece of immensely professional store-planning, but not architecture in the earlier sense.

The next stage of the development can be seen, still on Wilshire, just across Fairfax Avenue from May Company; Johnies, which actually does sell hamburgers. Somewhere underneath the fantasy lurks a plain rectangular flat-roofed building [53], around which a purely notional butterfly roof has been sketched, but turned down front and back to give a sheltering form not unlike the nominal mansard roofs that give the name to the Gourmet Mansardic style of restaurant architecture. On the front this roof is garnished with lettering, and the whole structure is flanked by entirely independent signs, one merely lettered, the other humorously [sic] pictorial. And a crowning non sequitur – an enormous sign which is part of the structure but advertises something entirely different.

53. Johnics Wilshire, Miracle Mile, 1962

The lower down the scales of financial substance and cultural pretensions one goes, the better sense it apparently makes (and has made, visibly, for a couple of decades) to buy a plain standard building shell from Butler Buildings Corporation or a similar mass-producer and add symbolic garnish to the front, top, or other parts that show. It makes even better sense, of course, to acquire an existing disused building and impose your commercial personality on it with symbolic garnishes. But even if you are a major commercial operator with a chain of outlets, even a major oil company, it still makes financial sense to put up relatively simple single-storey boxes, and then make them tall enough to attract attention by piling up symbols and graphic art on top. So Jack-in-the-Box heaps storey heights of graphics and symbols on top of quite simple and unassumingly functional drive-by hamburger

54. Norwalk Square shopping centre, Norwalk

bars; or a big supermarket may even run up an entirely independent sign detached from any building, and make it a visually interesting structure in its own right, like the double-tapered lattice tower at Norwalk Square [54].

But having proposed this sliding scale of commercial frugality versus cultural or aesthetic status, I have to admit some major anomalies that spoil the graph – though this is fair enough in the realm of fantasy. Many banks, despite their manifest status as monuments to the most enduring cultural values of a frankly acquisitive way of life, make a strong pitch at the Pop commercial level. Sometimes – as with the notorious applied art work of the Ahmanson Banks – it is possible to suspect such a confusion of cultural intentions as to make further discussion pointless (though no less humorous), but there are a few bank buildings which are designed exactly by the rules discussed above. The best example is the Cabrillo Savings Bank building on the Pacific Coast Highway at Torrance, which has a three-storey-high arcaded porch *à la* Yamasaki (for which the local source would be Ed Stone's Perpetual Savings Banks) and clearly functioning as a symbol of superior cultural tone, but entirely separate from the single-storey bank building around which it is wrapped, a total discrimination between the functional and symbolic parts of the design.

The other and more interesting area of anomalies embraces the architecture of restaurants, where these have any pretensions above the level of burger bars or coffee shops. There is a fairly well-defined middle level of domestic affluence in Los Angeles whose presence can be identified by certain key adjectives used in advertising to signify the kind of pretension that is also common in the middle rank of restaurants. These are *Custom* ('custom view homes'), *Decorator* ('antiqued decorator bar-stools'), and *Gourmet* ('gourmet party dips'). Within its own field the last has such precise status, outranking *Delicatessen* by the same degree that *Delicatessen* outranks *grocery*, that it seems entirely appropriate to adopt *Gourmet* as the stylistic label for the more aspiring kind of restaurant architecture.

From the Brown Derby onwards, through the Velvet Turtle at Redondo Beach, and onwards into a plushly under-lit future of 'Total Meal Experience', restaurants have been the most intensely and completely designed buildings in the area – few, even, of the most expensive houses can have had so much detailed attention devoted to them inside and out, and some of Rudolph Schindler's most inventive and advanced design was inside the Sardi's he did in 1932. In their current incarnations, they tend to be dark, both in terms of levels of illumination and the colour of woodwork, floor-coverings (often tiles or brick) and other integral surfaces, much subdivided by pierced screens or theatrically focused on a massive open fire-hearth or two.

This kind of Gourmet/Decorator interior is common in other parts of the US, of course; the Los Angeles variant differs in its greater reliance on Spanish Colonial sources (including one or two genuine pre-1848 pieces of furniture if possible) but chiefly in being done with greater skill, resourcefulness, and conviction. The same is true of the gourmet exterior in its two chief local varieties. The 'Gracious Living' variant often recalls the kind of nineteenth-century architecture that Professor Hitchcock categorized as 'Second Empire and Cognate Modes' slightly compromised by Hudson River Bracketted. To the front of the standard lightweight rectangular building shell this style adds round-arched openings, thin pretty detailing such as balconies and the small, steeply pitched false roof-fronts that justify the stylistic epithet Gourmet Mansardic.

The 'Char-broiled Protein' variant, on the other hand, has its ultimate sources in the ranch-house style, locally modified by the influence of the Greene Brothers and Frank Lloyd Wright, and shaggy surfaces that have the same implications of masculinity as an unshaven chin; massive rough-tiled roofs pulled well down and well out beyond the building envelope, exposed and roughly finished timber within and without, supplemented by random rubble or field-stone for exposed structural columns and the open hearths which are, of course, fundamental to the whole style – even to the extent of being supplemented by purely symbolic fire-pits under metal hoods on the outside of the building in some examples. Planning variations within the style extend from the endlessly informal to neatly balanced pairs of pavilions under 'mausoleum' roofs, Philadelphia-style, and the whole manner reaches one of its most notable local extremes in the so-called Polynesian restaurants.

In terms of geographical distribution, as well as stylistic pretensions, the Polynesians are everywhere from High-Gourmet 'Restaurant Row' next to Gallery Row on La Cienega Boulevard, to your local neighbourhood shopping centre. Epitomized by, say, the Tahitian Village in Bellflower [55], it exhibits a high, peaky roof pulled out

55. Tahitian Village restaurant, Bellflower, 1965

across the side-walk in a long pointed gable that must owe more, ultimately, to Saarinen's Hockey Rink than to anything in the South Seas, and a profusion of carved wood and rough hewn surfaces (even the risers of the external steps have been distressed with a trowel before the cement was dry) buried in a positive green salad of impenetrable exotic evergreens.

A building as strikingly and lovably ridiculous as this represents well enough the way Los Angeles sums up a general phenomenon of US life; the convulsions in building style that follow when traditional cultural and social restraints have been overthrown and replaced by the preferences of a mobile, affluent, consumer-oriented society, in which 'cultural values' and ancient symbols are handled primarily as methods of claiming or establishing status. This process has probably gone further in, say, Las Vegas, yet it is in the context of Los Angeles that everyone seems to feel the strongest compulsion to discuss this fantasticating tendency.

And rightly so. Until Las Vegas became unashamedly middle-aged and the boring Beaux-Arts Caesars' Palace was built, its architecture was an extreme suburban variant of Los Angeles – Douglas Honnold, now a respected doyen of the architectural profession in Los Angeles, worked for Bugsy Siegel in the design of the Flamingo, the pioneer casino-hotel on the Strip. Las Vegas has been as much a marginal gloss on Los Angeles as was Brighton Pavilion on Regency London. More important, Los Angeles has seen in this century the greatest concentration of fantasy-production, as an industry and as an institution, in the history of Western man. In the guise of Hollywood, Los Angeles gave us the movies as we know them and stamped its image on the infant television industry. And stemming from the impetus given by Hollywood as well as other causes, Los Angeles is also the home of the most extravagant myths of private gratification and self-realization, institutionalized now in the doctrine of 'doing your own thing'.

Both Hollywood's marketable commercial fantasies, and those private ones which are above or below calculable monetary value, have left their marks on the Angel City, but Hollywood brought something that all other fantasists needed – technical skill and resources in converting fantastic ideas into physical realities. Since living flesh-and-blood actors and dancers had to walk through or prance upon Hollywood's fantasies, there was much that could not be accomplished with painted back-cloths or back-projections; much of Shangri-la had to be built in three dimensions, the spiral ramps of the production numbers of Busby Berkeley musical spectaculars had to support the weight of a hundred girls in silver top hats, and so on . . .

The movies were thus a peerless school for building fantasy as fact, and the facts often survived one movie to live again in another, and another and others still to come. Economy in using increasingly valuable acreage on studio-lots caused these fantastic façades and ancient architectures reproduced in plaster to be huddled together into what have become equally fantastic townscapes which not only survive as cities of romantic illusion [56], but have been elevated to

56. Universal City film-lot

57a. The lake, Disneyland

the status of a kind of cultural monuments, which now form the basis for tourist excursions more flourishing than the traditional tours of film-stars' homes.

This business of showing the plant to visitors as a tourist attraction has spread beyond the movie industry, into such monuments of public relations as the Busch Gardens in the San Fernando Valley, where the real-life brewery is only one of the features shown, and back into the movie industry with Disneyland – the set for a film that was never ever going to be made except in the mind of the visitor. In creating this compact sequence of habitable fantasies, WED Enterprises seem to have transcended Hollywood, Los Angeles, Walt Disney's original talents and all other identifiable ingredients of this environmental phantasmagoria.

In terms of an experience one can walk or ride through, inhabit and enjoy, it is done with such consummate skill and such base cunning that one can only compare it to something completely outrageous, like the brothel in Genet's *Le Balcon*. It is an almost faultless organization for delivering, against cash, almost any type at all of environmental experience that human fancy, however inflamed, could ever devise [57 a, b]. Here are pedestrian piazzas, seas, jungles, castles, outer space, Main Street, the old West, mountains, more than can be experienced in a single day's visit . . . and all embraced within some obvious ironies, as all institutionalized fantasies must be.

The greatest of these ironies has to do with transportation, and this underlies the brothel comparison. Set in the middle of a city obsessed with mobility, a city whose most characteristic festival is the Rose Parade in Pasadena, fantastically sculptured Pop inventions entirely surfaced with live flowers rolling slowly down Colorado Boulevard every New Year's Day – in this city Disneyland offers illicit pleasures of mobility. Ensconced in a sea of giant parking-lots in a city devoted to the automobile, it provides transportation that does not exist outside – steam trains, monorails, people-movers,

57b. Transportation fantasy, Disneyland

tram-trains, travelators, ropeways, not to mention pure transport fantasies such as simulated space-trips and submarine rides. Under-age children, too young for driver's licences, enjoy the licence of driving on their own freeway system and adults can step off the pavement and mingle with the buses and trams on Main Street in a manner that would lead to sudden death or prosecution outside.

But more than this, the sheer concentration of different forms of mechanical movement means that Disneyland is almost the only place where East Coast town-planning snobs, determined that their cities shall never suffer the automotive 'fate' of Los Angeles, can bring their students or their city councillors to see how the alternative might work in the flesh and metal – to this blatantly commercial fun-fair in the city they hate. And seeing how well it all worked, I began to understand the wisdom of Ray Bradbury in proposing that Walt Disney was the only man who could make rapid transit a success in Los Angeles. All the skill, cunning, salesmanship, and technical proficiency are there.

They are also at diametrical variance with the special brand of 'innocence' that underlies the purely personal fantasies of Los Angeles. Innocence is a word to use cautiously in this context, because it must be understood as not comprising either simplicity or ingenuousness. Deeply imbued with standard myths of the Natural Man and the Noble Savage, as in other parts of the US, this innocence grows and flourishes as an assumed right in the Southern California sun, an ingenious and technically proficient cult of private and harmless gratifications that is symbolized by the surfer's secret smile of intense concentration and the immensely sophisticated and highly decorated plastic surf-board he needs to conduct his private communion with the sea.

This fantasy of innocence has one totally self-absorbed and perfected monument in Los Angeles, so apt, so true and so imaginative that it has gained the world-wide fame it undoubtedly deserves: Simon Rodia's clustered towers in Watts. Alone of the buildings of Los Angeles they are almost too well known to need description, tapering traceries of coloured pottery shards [58a, b] bedded in cement on frames of scrap steel and baling wire. They are unlike anything else in the world – especially unlike all the various prototypes that have been proposed for them by historians who have never seen them in physical fact. Their actual presence is testimony to a genuinely original creative spirit.

And in the thirty-three years of absorbed labour he devoted to their construction, and in his uninhibited ingenuity in exploiting the by-products of an affluent technology, and in his determination to 'do something big', and in his ability to walk away when they were finished in 1954, Rodia was very much at one with the surfers, hot-rodders, sky-divers, and scuba-divers who personify the tradition of private, mechanistic *satori*-seeking in California. But he was also at variance with the general body of fantastic architecture thereabouts.

58a, b. Watts Towers, 1921–54, Simon Rodia, inventor

Architecture as a way of direct personal gratification like Rodia's rarely rises above the level of plaster-gnomery or home-is-where-the-heart-shaped-flower-bed-is [59]. The towers of Watts are as unique as they are proper in Los Angeles, for the going body of architectural

59. Home is where the (do-it-yourself) heart is

fantasy is in the public, not private, domain, and constitutes almost the only public architecture in the city – public in the sense that it deals in symbolic meanings the populace at large can read. Both fantasy and public symbolism reached their apotheosis in the great commercial signs, in the style of design that Tom Wolfe acclaimed, in his own neologism, as 'electrographic architecture' – that is, a combination of artificial light and graphic art that can even comprise a whole building. Wolfe's chosen examples in Los Angeles are the Crenshaw Ford Agency [60] and the Crenshaw Mobil Station in which he sees, rightly, a move 'from mere lettering to whole structures designed primarily as

60. Crenshaw Ford Agency, 1967

pictures or representational sculpture'. Wild as these objects may appear, grotesque, ludicrous, stimulating or uplifting, they fit into an established local pattern of architectural invention that reaches deep into the city's history and style of life.

Historically, the tradition begins with the spires, not of Watts but of Westwood village: illuminated needles capping cinemas and even banks in order to be seen from Wilshire Boulevard, which is only a quarter of a mile away, but which was not (in the twenties, when Westwood was subdivided) zoned for commercial uses. And this tradition also crowns the city's life-style, not only in commercial signs, but also in one structure that is a public building in the conventional sense of the word, the only public building in the whole city that genuinely graces the scene and lifts the spirit (and sits in firm control of the whole basis of human existence in Los Angeles): the Water and Power Building [61] of 1964 by Albert C. Martin and Associates. In daylight it is a conventional rectangular office block closing the end of an uninspired civic vista and standing in an altogether ordinary pool full of the usual fountains, but at night it is transformed. Darkness hides the boredoms of the civic centre and from the flanking curves of the freeways one sees only this brilliant cube of diamond-cool light riding above the lesser lights of downtown. It is the only gesture of public architecture that matches the style and scale of the city.

61. Water and Power Building, Los Angeles Civic Centre, 1963,
Albert C. Martin and Associates, architects

7 The Art of the Enclave

Planning in Los Angeles? In the world's eyes this is a self-cancelling concept. And the world is right, coarsely speaking – very coarsely speaking indeed, for this has always been a planned city; Lieutenant Ord's survey map of 1849 is also a plan for further development, and there has been enough town planning since then to fill a thick cyclostyled historical report submitted to the Mayor in 1964. And after the Report there was a major attempt to take town planning to the people after Calvin Hamilton became planner to the City in 1965 – the Los Angeles Goals Program intended to involve the citizens in fundamental decisions about the future of the area.

But before the Goals Program could even begin to move, it was necessary to explain to the citizenry what town planning was, and exemplify rock-bottom concepts like High and Low Density in words and pictures little above primary school standards of sophistication (*Concepts for Los Angeles*, 1967). Such evidence of the small impact of planning on the life and consciousness of Angelenos, after sixty years of effort, was a deep disappointment to good dedicated men and true who genuinely wished to work for what they conceived to be a fairer Los Angeles. Now even the Goals Program has quietly withered away, leaving behind little more than the proposal that the city shall develop much as it has in the recent past – clusters of towers in a sea of single family dwellings.

The situation is not as desperate as some professional planners might feel. The failure-rate of town planning is so high throughout the world that one can only marvel that the profession has not long since given up trying; the history of the art of planning is a giant wastebin of sumptuously forgotten paper projects. Nor does the sixty-year chronicle of planning in Los Angeles mean that vast human and financial resources have been squandered – in 1910 the City made an appropriation of $100 (count them, one hundred!) for the Planning Committee; in 1963–4 the appropriation touched 1½ million, which was hardly gigantic for a major metropolis allegedly in the throes of a planning crisis, and with an assessed valuation of $5,419,077,933.

Psychologically, the nub of the matter seems to be that planning, as the discipline is normally understood in academic and professional circles, is one of those admired facets of the established Liberal approach to urban problems that has never struck root in the libertarian, but illiberal, atmosphere of Los Angeles (whatever pockets of conventional

62. Commercial non-plan on Sepulveda Boulevard

good planning may have been created by local pockets of conventional liberal thinking). Indeed, it is so much a stranger that one feels it could even do harm. While conventional planners are almost certainly right in asserting that without planning Los Angeles *might* destroy itself, the fact remains that conventional planning wisdom certainly *would* destroy the city as we know it.

Take the supposed problem of 'visual pollution by commercial advertising' [62]. Planning propagandists who use the phrase do themselves and their cause no good; it suggests that pollution is only a question of cultural taste, and thus tends to trivialize the problem of chemical pollution which attacks human beings at a direct physiological level. But more than this, anyone who cares for the unique character of individual cities must see that the proliferation of advertising signs is an essential part of the character of Los Angeles; to deprive the city of them would be like depriving San Gimignano of its towers or the City of London of its Wren steeples. And by the sound of conversations around the world, the point is now recognized; orthodox city planners who fulminate against the signs are now outnumbered not only by those who are indifferent to them, but – more significantly – by those who find something to admire in them, their flamboyance, and the constant novelty induced by their obsolescence and replacement.

Conventional standards of planning do not work in Los Angeles, and it feels more natural (I put it no stronger than that) to leave the effective planning of the area to the mechanisms that have already given the city its present character: the infrastructure to giant agencies like the Division of Highways and the Metropolitan Water District and their like; the intermediate levels of management to the subdivision and zoning ordinances; the detail decisions to local and private initiatives; with *ad hoc* interventions by city, State, and pressure-groups formed to agitate over matters of clear and present need. These are the mechanisms which are seen and known to be effective by the man in

the family station wagon (or whatever the local equivalent of the Clapham omnibus may be).

This is not to claim that any of these mechanisms is any more perfect than any other human institution, or works more than averagely well. The Division of Highways (a State body, incidentally) notoriously tends to behave with all the sensitivity of a rogue dinosaur, but its lumbering progress can be exploited for the public good at times – in attempting to create park-strips in Watts, for instance. Bending the zoning regulations is reckoned to be a bigger area of graft than the vice industry, since changes in zoning directly affect land-values and thus impinge on the oldest Angeleno method of turning a fast buck. So, while zoning changes threaten the ancient monuments of modern architecture on King's Road, they are also to be thanked for the creation of the prototype linear downtown on Wilshire Boulevard [63], threaded through its catchment area of residential zones.

Outside the administrative area of the City of Los Angeles itself, the other communities that make up Greater Los Angeles (up to sixty of them if your view is Greater enough) have their own views on the meaning and purpose of zoning practices, and in some cases they have drafted them, and employed them, to reinforce local town-planning layouts of the kind that professional planners have, indeed, prepared – but usually without any nonsense about planning being for the good of the public at large. In Los Angeles a master-plan and the legislation to make it effective are most likely to be found in incorporated cities of an exclusively middle-class make-up who are determined to stay exclusive. The apotheosis of such closed communities is ' . . . the unique city of Rolling Hills . . . which consists entirely of three square miles of country estates, completely enclosed by white-rail fencing and entered only through four guarded gates', as Augusta Fink put it. Having been turned back by the guard at one of these gates in pouring rain at a time when other ways across Palos Verdes were blocked by landslips, I find it fairly easy to understand how these enclosed and planned communities are found unsympathetic by local libertarians.

To be fair, Augusta Fink's real topic, the 'terraced land' of the adjoining city of Palos Verdes proper, is less neurotically enclosed and has a far more interesting plan, and is more representative of the general aims of planned communities in the area. Incorporated as a city only in 1939, it had been in process of creation since the early twenties, to a design by Albert Olmsted and Frederick Olmsted II (sons of the great park planner) and the architect Myron C. Hunt. The plan, in fact, runs over into the adjoining city of Torrance,

64. Malaga Cove Plaza, Palos Verdes, 1925 onwards

incorporated in 1921, and the difference in generation (and type of population) shows most clearly in the trees – in Torrance their distribution is about normal for an uncontrolled development, but in Palos Verdes not only can you not see the wood for the trees, you can't see the planning either. Hunt's axial flights of steps from terrace to terrace are almost invisible. Clearly, trees have a special status in Palos Verdes; they come under the combined protection of the Palos Verdes Homes Association and the Palos Verdes Art Jury, which together watch over the maintenance of the social, economic, and environmental character of the city. The planting is almost entirely artificial and recent – photographs of the little piazza at Malaga Cove

65. California City, Mojave, 1963, Smith and Williams, planners

[64] in the early twenties show barely enough trees to count; now the arcaded Spanish Colonial Revival shops stand in an inhabited forest.

There is yet another Angeleno irony here; the most prestigious and professional piece of planning in the area has been swamped and buried by the general determination to maintain the illusion of living in homesteads set in primal verdure, an illusion now fixed and institutionalized by conservatively applied regulations. Less ironical and less humorous is the concern expressed by serious and devoted Paloverdan parents at the unbalance of their community and its facilities, which they feel put teenagers at risk of delinquency – reckoned to be a general failing of planned communities of what might be considered the middle generation.

Older communities have tended to balance up through attrition of the original planning intentions; younger ones tend to claim a degree of social balance, and balance in provision of facilities, among their initial planning intentions. The remoter ones, like California City on the high desert [65], Valencia on the Newhall (San Francisco) Rancho at the head of the San Fernando Valley, or Westlake at the valley's western extremity . . . these, typically, make claims to balance in their way of life, but it is interesting that these claims depend less on the provision of the kind of institutional facilities (schools, etc.) that might be expected, than on the creation of open-air installations for recreation.

Traditionally, such provisions were country clubs, with or without a golf course – as at Bel Air, for instance. But in the newer and remoter instances, an artificial body of water is almost mandatory. Westlake takes its name from a central artificial lake (whose contents appear to be a bone of contention with neighbouring agricultural interests) while California City's central lake seems, in its improbable desert setting, both ludicrous enough to be a joke, and welcome enough to be a blessed miracle. Even newer desert cities, like those projected for the area south of Barstow, make an even stronger sales pitch of their lakes – and a much less likeable one.

Emphasizing the growing pressure on recreational facilities as California's population mushrooms, they make a frankly alarmist appeal: 'Did you know that within a decade visits by Americans to Government-owned recreation areas may have to be rationed on the basis of one every five to ten years . . . make reservations three years in advance . . . by 1985 reservations will be needed to have a picnic in the neighbourhood park . . .' Ignoring the possibility of new provisions by State, County, or City, the advertisers offer private-membership lakes as the only solution, either as the focus of the new settlement, with a residential qualification for membership, or even, apparently, in extreme cases, with access to the water only from shoreline residential plots (as has happened accidentally at Malibu).

So recreational living tends to become another synonym for the social 'turf' system of closed communities; systematic planning remains the creation of privileged enclaves. Less frequently it has meant the creation of underprivileged enclaves, since much of the

66. Baldwin Hills Village, 1938, Clarence Stein, planning consultant

residential planning of the late thirties, for instance, was intended to create tidy places to dispose of socially untidy people, the lower working classes as understood in the political dogma of the time. Ramona Village and Carmelitos, both of 1939, were public authority projects of this kind for which Clarence Stein of Radburn fame was a consultant – as he was also for the distinctly *non*-working-class Baldwin Hills Village [66] of the same period, originally promoted by the subdividers of the Rancho Cienega o Paso de la Tijera under the more typically Angeleno name of 'Thousand Gardens'. Within a couple more years, with the war about to break out, this kind of residential planning became a matter of urgency to house the influx of new industrial workers. Of these emergency settlements the most distinguished and best-known, of course, is Richard Neutra's Channel Heights [67], and

67. Channel Heights housing, San Pedro, 1942, Richard Neutra, architect

a little of its architectural quality has sometimes rubbed off on subsequent exercises in 'Project Housing' – but most of this work is unlovely enough to deserve the stigma that attaches to 'livin' in the projects'.

But to revert to the older communities; the under-equipment complained of in Palos Verdes is, to some extent, a product of its being laid out in the first flush of automobilistic enthusiasms, and this probably goes for other middle-generation communities. You can, in theory, get in the car and go to find what you need. Remote newer suburbs cannot really pretend to this because of their remoteness; the earlier ones could not because of the absence of automobiles – Pacific Electric Railroad notwithstanding. So Beverly Hills, though an effectively closed community in terms of social class, still embraces a variety of functions, and feels less claustrophobic than some later communities.

As a development case-history, Beverly Hills displays a satisfying neatness of execution; a complete Rancho – the Rodeo de Las Aguas – was laid out in 1906 by a single company, the Rodeo Land and Water Company, to the designs of a single planner, Wilbur Cook, specially brought in from New York. In 1914, with a few additions to its acreage, it was incorporated as a single city, capable of being armed with the necessary ordinances to defend its social make-up and rather arty standards of design.

By a splendid paradox, its defensive social legislation, intended to keep out the underprivileged or undecorous, was for years administered through a socialist mayor – the irreplaceable Will Rogers, and in spite of all its careful organization and tidy planning, the success of the whole project probably depended more than anything on the Fairbanks/Pickford household deciding to move there.

In spite of its affluent exclusivism, Beverly Hills does include a sizeable area of non-residential business and commercial development, embracing as it does both Santa Monica and Wilshire Boulevards

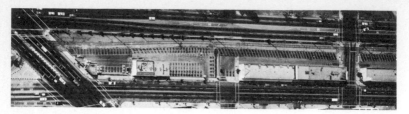

68. Beverly Hills at Wilshire and Santa Monica Boulevards

[68] for a short distance of their total lengths. But quite typically of Wilbur Cook's original intentions and their later interpretation, there is a continuous strip of tree-planting or ornamental shrubs to conceal the railway line along the side of Santa Monica Boulevard, and after the railway declined and the boulevard itself became heavily trafficked, the house-plots fronting on the boulevard were cleared and put down to open grass while the houses pulled back behind yet another defensive line of shrubs – residential illusions must be defended against the facts of the life that makes them possible.

The adjoining Rancho San José de Buenos Aires presents a different picture. Almost twenty years younger, it is much less obviously designed and represents a more diversified and less defensive kind of basic subdivision approach. Earlier attempts to subdivide had failed (Sunset City) and much of the rancho remained leased agricultural lands – a beanfield survived in my time – until after it passed out of Wolfskill ownership and into the hands of Arthur Letts in 1919, and the regents of the University of California had been persuaded to locate their Los Angeles campus in the middle of it in 1925 (and not, for instance, at Palos Verdes, also a short-listed site). So, while David Allison laid out the nucleus of the present UCLA campus [69] and designed its extraordinary Lombardic buildings, the Janss Brothers set about subdividing the rest on behalf of the Letts estates.

Because its annexation to the City of Los Angeles proper effectively prevents any specially restrictive zoning beyond what can be built into individual sets of title deeds, the present development on the old Wolfskill ranch has a much less closed-in air than even Beverly Hills – to which it is in some senses a slightly decadent successor, since the Holmby Hills section was the legendary stamping ground of the film colony's notorious Holmby Hills Rat-pack. The UCLA campus is inevitably public property to which all classes and conditions of Angelenos must be able to come for university and extension courses, day and night, so there is a constant coming and going which underlines the sense of open access. But more than this, the campus creates a special kind of residential demand which almost makes special zoning unnecessary. Because academics apparently drive much less (here, if not at the older University of Southern California) than most

69. Westwood Village and UCLA campus in 1929

Angelenos, there seems to be a solid and insatiable demand for certain grades of middle-class accommodation (from professorial mansions down to Ph.D. apartments) that make the areas near the campus pretty well stable socially.

Nevertheless, the old rancho contains two areas more conspicuously planned than the rest: Bel Air with its labyrinthine layout behind the inevitably Spanish Colonial Revival of its entrance gates; and the model shopping centre of Westwood Village. This too is Spanish Colonial Revival (like its contemporary, Carthay Circle, in Beverly Hills, now wiped out by the new offices of the Victor Gruen organ-

70. Westwood *paseo*

ization) but the style was very simple. Westwood too has suffered since it was built, being punched out by parking-lots (the Janss Brothers seem to have foreseen the motor age less accurately than Ross on Miracle Mile), and invaded by giant office blocks made possible by changes in zoning regulations. But the triangular central *paseo* [70] remains almost undisturbed, deliciously small in scale with its peeling whitewashed brick walls, its circular corner towers, tiled roofs, and minute, cool, internal courtyards with vines and balconies. Among all those filling-stations and within sight of the traffic on Wilshire, it's another planned illusion – but it belongs to a class of illusions that persists long locally, and pervades the newest wave of enclave planning: the creation of pedestrian spaces.

It may sound an odd preoccupation for a city apparently given over body and soul to the automobile, but it has been going on since before the motor age, and the automobile has added new impetus to it now. Long before the automobile became a problem, the city had tended to produce small courtyard plans for domestic and business purposes. Irving Gill's Lewis Courts at Sierra Madre is a good early example, so was Arthur Heineman's Los Robles bungalow precinct in Pasadena of 1910. So is the court off Western Avenue where the painter Ed Ruscha has his studio, of indeterminate age and architectural detailing, but environmentally admirable with its central tree. The ocean pleasure piers have been impregnable pedestrian fortresses in most cases, so was the Pike at Long Beach, so is the concrete walkway that separates so many miles of beach from the city behind, and 'Gallery Row' on La Cienega is the venue for a mandatory promenade on Monday nights, the approved time for *vernissages*.

But the crucial type of pedestrian precinct in this context is the commercial shopping Mall, a tradition that begins with the regularization and pedestrianization of Olvera Street [71], north of the Plaza (but probably not the site of the original pueblo), in 1929. What started there as a civic gesture is now little more than a tourist trap,

71. Olvera Street

but it is a very good and colourful tourist trap, and many of the flanking buildings are genuinely as old as they look. Questions of genuineness are not the point however. The point is that Olvera Street manages to deliver all those qualities of animation and spontaneity which few professional planners can achieve with the best will in the world.

At this level, pedestrian shopping plazas are one of the better features of the Los Angeles area. Not all of them; some are only parking-lots with pretensions. The parking-lot component in these pedestrian plans is not to be despised, however, since the resolution of where to put the car has a great deal to do with the eventual location of the pedestrian. Early car-dominated shopping-centre designs like Victor Gruen's Westchester scheme [72] with its roof-top parking and crossed Futurist ramps leading up to it, imposed an over-compact

72. Westchester Shopping Centre, 1950,
Victor Gruen Associates, architects and planners

pattern that might have made better sense somewhere more short of space. Almost two decades later, the shopping centre at Century City inverts the physical priorities, puts multi-level car parks below and puts the pedestrian piazza on top, a solution which enables the shopping to be broken up into smaller units, around which the shopper can perambulate.

The intermediate stages between these two schemes are not only, nor significantly, the kind of theorizing about piazza-planning that had been going on in Europe and in U S architecture schools. The important inter-mediate stage seems to be Gruen's experience elsewhere, and other people's experience in Los Angeles, as in Farmers' Market, with an uninhibited type of one-level design. Putting the parking and the shopping on the same level made it possible to expand the shopping facility as demand increased. It also made it possible to stir up the shopping and the parking more intimately, so that the long walk across the parking-lot could end sooner – and in the process, almost by inattention, the central pedestrian mall [73] among the shops emerged. Inattention did not last long; some of the best 'civic design' – seats, planting, fountains, fancy paving – in the Los Angeles area is to be found in shopping centres.

These shopping centres are also Internal Combustion City's alternative to Main Street, the natural foci of a highly mobile population that measures distance in time at the wheel. But the techniques of

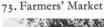
73. Farmers' Market

74. Burbank Mall (beautiful downtown Burbank), 1968,
Simon Eisner and Lyle Stewart, architects and planners

75. Riverside Mall, 1966,
Ruhnau, Evans and Steinman, architects and planners

design evolved for their central pedestrian spaces have now begun to come to the rescue of Main Street itself. The rehabilitation of older subsidiary downtown areas, by bringing them up to shopping-centre standards, has become one of the more attractive aspects of enclave planning. However dominant the automobile and its associated lobbies may appear, it is probably easier to close off a street in Los Angeles as a pedestrian preserve than it is in most English cities, and the resulting traffic-free space provides an excellent arena for a profitable interplay of commercial enterprise and municipal improvement.

Thus the current joke that has made Downtown Burbank an international byword, depends on the fact that the area has been made as beautiful as institutional action can make it, in contrast to the surrounding blight and industrial mess that is all the casual freeway-borne visitor is likely to see there. Almost a mile of San Fernando Road has been pedestrianized and lavishly fitted out with civic tackle and trees [74], while the original Main Street shops (or their equivalents) survive on either side, suitably smartened up, with vast parking-lots behind. In other words, this is the next step beyond Wilshire Boulevard: a linear *pedestrian* motorized downtown.

Since this kind of conversion-urbanism must always be largely at the mercy of the surviving buildings and existing shops on either side of the pedestrian space, the overall success of these malls is variable. Santa Monica Mall tries very hard, but the adjoining struc-tures are very undistinguished; Riverside Mall, on the other hand, starts with an advantage so enormous as to be almost unfair, flanked as it is by the flying buttresses and arcading of Arthur Benton's ultimate monument of the Mission-style wing of the Spanish Colonial Revival, the incredible Mission Inn hotel. Already penetrated by pedestrian routes, arcades, and courtyards of a semi-public nature, the Mission Inn provides a natural nucleus from which the Mall can extend into the public domain [75], so that the oldest and newest fantasies of the good life in Southern California – the resort hotel and the pedestrian mall

– meet and run together to form a civic centre and an urban illusion that any city of the New World could envy.

But mention of Spanish Colonial Revival fantasies calls to mind two planned communities that are among the most naturally likeable areas of all Los Angeles. They are of the same generation and type: waterborne seaside communities of the early 1900s. One is Naples, east of Long Beach, in the form of an oval island with an internal canal, sitting in the landlocked harbour of Alamitos Bay. Subdivided by A. M. Parsons in 1903, with a posh hotel by Almira Hershey of Hollywood Hotel fame, it survived the earthquake of 1933, and is now a slightly somnolent canalside community [76] (with good modern houses by Soriano, and by Killingsworth–Brady–Smith) balanced

76. Naples, 1903 onwards

around a green mall that runs back from the water to terminate in a small palm-grove surrounding a single unexplained Roman Doric column.

The other is romantically blighted Venice. Decreed by Abbott Kinney in 1905, it created a dream city [77] of gondolas, bridges, and lagoons out of the squaggy sands and marshes south of Santa Monica. The overall layout was the work of Norman and Robert

Marsh, who also designed public structures like the ornate canal-bridges, and some uninhibited private houses. It must have been a splendid vision – but in 1927 oil was struck there and fantasy had to give way to fact.

When I first saw it, bridges wrapped in barbed wire (because they were dangerous) spanned a single slimy canal among abandoned oil machinery and nodding pumps that were still at work. Desolation was

77 (*opposite*). Venice, from the pier, 1905

78. Venice, the arcades of Windward Avenue

everywhere, except where a narrow strip of houses still straggled down the ocean beach, and where two or three blocks of the original arcaded shopping street still survived on Windward Avenue. Those arcaded fragments [78] are perhaps the most affecting Romantic relics in the whole instant city, convincingly Mediterranean with their whitewashed walls and brightly painted capitals to the columns. The district is run-down still, something between a ghetto and a hippie haven, with social problems on both counts, but on a Sunday morning under the stunning early sunlight with couples (not always heterosexual) strolling past under the colonnades on their way to get the papers, or a bottle of something, or just to exercise the dog, you can see why this area, above all others, attracts the kind of Angeleno who needs or prefers a basically European type of city. Kinney's dream has come true to that extent – but may not long survive the impending avalanche of affluent aspiring house-owners who are just discovering the abundance of attractive building sites along the banks of the rehabilitated canals.

8 Ecology III: The Plains of Id

The world's image of Los Angeles (as opposed to its images of component parts like Hollywood or Malibu) is of an endless plain endlessly gridded with endless streets, peppered endlessly with ticky-tacky houses clustered in indistinguishable neighbourhoods, slashed across by endless freeways that have destroyed any community spirit that may once have existed, and so on . . . endlessly. Statistically and superficially this might be a fair picture if Los Angeles consisted only of the problem areas of the City proper, the small percentage of the total metropolis that urban alarmists delight to dwell upon. But even though it is an untrue picture on any fair assessment of the built structure and the topography of the Greater Los Angeles area, there is a certain underlying psychological truth about it – in terms of some of the most basic and unlovely but vital drives of the urban psychology of Los Angeles, the flat plains are indeed the heartlands of the city's Id [79].

These central flatlands are where the crudest urban lusts and most fundamental aspirations are created, manipulated and, with luck, satisfied. In so far as the history of Los Angeles is a story of the unscrupulous and profitable subdivision of land, for instance, from the initial breaking up of the Spanish land grants to their final platting-out into their present occupied lots, the plains are where it most spectacularly happened and where the craftiest techniques of sale were worked out, and where the most psychotic forms of territorial posses-sion (armed Rightists in Orange County preparing to shoot down victims of atomic attack) dirty-up the pretty dream of urban home-steading out of which most of Los Angeles has been built.

These characteristic patterns of land manipulation did not really originate, however, in the central areas most often illustrated to show the horrors of Los Angeles. It was to the east, in the San Gabriel

79. Map of the Los Angeles plains areas

Valley, the area traversed by the rail and road links to San Bernardino, that much of its style and history can still be seen by the traveller on the Berdoo or – better – Foothill Boulevard, which keeps mostly just below the foothills, on the plain proper. Here, the land, traversed by erratic streams from the hills, was cultivable without importing water

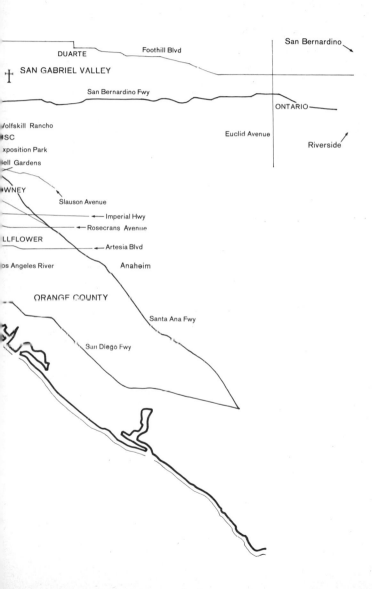

miles

0   2   4   6   8   10

San Bernardino

DUARTE   Foothill Blvd

SAN GABRIEL VALLEY

San Bernardino Fwy   ONTARIO

Wolfskill Rancho
SC   Euclid Avenue
Exposition Park   Riverside
Bell Gardens

DOWNEY
                  Slauson Avenue
                         ← Imperial Hwy
                         ← Rosecrans Avenue
BELLFLOWER
                         ← Artesia Blvd

Los Angeles River   Anaheim

ORANGE COUNTY

                         Santa Ana Fwy

                  San Diego Fwy

80. Mission San Gabriel, etching by H. C. Ford, 1883

from far away, hence the establishment of the Mission San Gabriel [80] in the broad valley-bottom, out of which it conjured prodigies of fertility – measured against the agronomy of the time, if not against present standards.

Further east, in 1851, the first commercial breaking up of rancho lands was begun by Henry Dalton, successful claimant to lands in San Francisquito and Azusa, almost as soon as his patents were confirmed; 9,000 acres in small farming plots, plus the promise of a townsite when trade warranted it (thought to correspond to the present Duarte). This was a real pioneer proposal, since the really big operators did not swing into operation until almost fifteen years later, when two of the inheritors of the San Antonio ranch disposed of their shares for subdivision, and Governor Downey began the subdivision of the Santa Gertrudes ranch, creating the present city of Downey in 1865.

The real rush to subdivide did not begin until another two decades later, when competition between the Southern Pacific and the Santa Fé Railroads brought the settlers flooding in, and provided the transportation base without which most subdivision would not have been viable. For the full pattern of subdivision required three things:

land that could economically be improved, water to make it support men and agriculture, and transportation to take men in and bring agricultural produce out. The soil of the San Gabriel was ideal for improvement because it could hardly get worse – a soft sand which supports a light desert scrub when left to its own devices, and turns into a kind of dry quicksand when broken for cultivation. But, watered, it grew corn for the Mission padres, beans, vines, olives and citrus fruits for the later intensive commercial farmers [81].

For much of its length, Foothill Boulevard traverses land still devoted to this pattern of agriculture: solid orchards of orange trees, though these are migrating to the slopes to get above the frost, and the

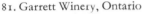
81. Garrett Winery, Ontario

baroque, contorted stumps of close-cropped vines in endless rows. Lines of eucalyptus (introduced in 1875) along the highways, as frost stops as much as windbreaks, and close groves of mingled palms, olives, eucalyptus, oaks and what have you around the farmhouses – which have often disappeared but left these miniature arboreta behind.

Even in its early stages, this was an agriculture that needed transportation as much as it needed water – Edwin Thomas Earl of the California Fruit Express had his first refrigerated rail-car away east in 1890 but, well before that, the first carload of California oranges had left for St Louis from a loading dock right inside the old Wolfskill orange groves at the western extremity of the San Gabriel Valley. The great German vineyards down at Anaheim, also, needed the railroads badly enough for an Anaheim spur to be part of the original package deal that brought the SP to Los Angeles. The rails still lace the plain as far east as San Bernardino and Riverside, where the motorist seems to bump over half-buried metal at every other intersection.

82. Ontario: Euclid Avenue in 1883

83 (*opposite*). Mission San Fernando as it is now

It was also in these eastern plains that commuting over long distances began, if we can trust Juan José Warner's testimony. In any case there is circumstantial evidence in support of this claim to primacy in the incredible statistic that at the peak of the land and railway boom of the mid eighties, there were no fewer than twenty-five real or figmentary townsites laid out along the thirty-six mile run of the Santa Fé between the pueblo and the San Bernardino county line. Precious few of them survive, and the most interesting of the survivors lies, in fact, the Berdoo side of the county line – Ontario.

Carved out of the Rancho Cucamonga in the early 1880s, Ontario [82] is as instructive as it is interesting. It is, even now, the city of fruit with streets named 'Sultana' and even 'Sunkist' in honour of the local products, and it still preserves the almost ludicrous grandeur of its original layout, with the impossibly broad double street – Euclid Avenue – bisecting it from north to south and crossing the railroad at a point still hopefully referred to as 'downtown'. Near the railroad, a

few early downtown-type buildings can be distantly perceived through the luxuriant tree-planting down the central reservation of Euclid, and also one or two vacant lots that look like they might have been there since the foundation of the city – the general impression is that the citizens of Ontario built a 'garden city' and left out the 'city' part, urban homesteaders imposing their ideal of suburbs without *urbs* on the pattern of Greater Los Angeles almost before it had begun to take shape, a portent of the way the whole metropolis would grow.

Within degrees, the opening up and subdivision of the San Fernando Valley, and of Orange County have been similar, though more stream-lined operations – especially the San Fernando [83], which has been a kind of big-speculator paradise ever since William Mulholland brought the water to the valley in 1913. As the water surged down the aqueduct, Mulholland made his most famous speech: 'There it is, take it!' He could equally well have been referring to the land of the valley itself, except that the big operators had already moved in without waiting for the water. The Los Angeles Suburban Homes Company (Harry Chandler and Harrison Gray Otis, of the Los Angeles *Times*, Moses 'General' Sherman, and others) had acquired 'Tract 1000' – 47,500 acres of dry wheatland in the southern part of the valley – as early as 1909, precipitating a pattern of development that has left most of the valley an intricate patchwork of agricultural and residential uses.

Broad, rather vague roads traverse these patterns, not vague as to their direction, which normally relates directly to the four compass points on an extremely regular grid, but vague as to their status and destination. A substantial four-lane highway will apparently stop at a white fence and a grove of trees, but will be found to have merely narrowed at an unwidened two-lane bridge over a dry wash, the trees marking the line of the stream; or the trees may stand on the property line of a farm-holding that has not yet been bought back for widening. In either case, the road may, or may not, return to full width after the interruption. Or again a road may suddenly come to a dead stop against a couple of mighty black irrigation tanks, indicating a still-undisturbed agricultural holding, on the far side of which, maybe a mile away, the road may or may not resume its straight course. Ultimately, such anomalies in the development pattern will be regularized, but at present they are more characteristic than any building type of the San Fernando Valley, and distinguish its ecology sharply from that of the plains south of the Santa Monica Mountains, the real heartland of the plains of Id.

These 'real' flatlands occupy the valley-bottoms of the rivers and creeks that drained the pre-historic Gulf of Los Angeles – valleys so broad-bottomed, rivers and creeks so indeterminate that they could change course cataclysmically after earthquakes, and have done so in historical times, draining swamps and emptying the few surviving lakes. These are the plains that are seen in the classic view south from the Griffith Park Observatory, and this view [84] does indeed show an endless flat city – the interminable parallels of Vermont, Normandie and Western Avenues stretching south as far as the eye can penetrate the urban haze, intersecting at absolutely precise right angles the east–west parallels of Hollywood, Sunset and Santa Monica Boulevards, Melrose Avenue, Beverly Boulevard, Third Street, Wilshire Boulevard, under the San Mo freeway, past Exposition Park and the campus of the University of Southern California and ever south, across Slauson, Florence, Manchester, Century, Imperial . . . on a clear day – a *very* clear day – the visible geometry extends twenty-odd miles to San Pedro.

It is, without doubt, one of the world's great urban vistas – and also one of the most daunting. Its sheer size, and sheer lack of quality in most of the human environments it traverses, mark it down

84 (*overleaf*). The view south from Griffith Park

169

85. Townscape in Watts

almost inevitably, as the area of problems like Watts [85], which lies
only a couple of miles east of the very midpoint of the Normandie
Avenue axis. In addition the great size and lack of distinction of the
area covered by this prospect make it the area where Los Angeles is
least distinctively itself. One of the reasons why the great plains of Id
are so daunting is that this is where Los Angeles is most like other
cities: Anywheresville/Nowheresville. Here, on Slauson Avenue, or
Rosecrans or the endless mileage of Imperial Highway, little beyond
the occasional palm-tree distinguishes the townscape from that of

Kansas City or Denver or Indianapolis. Here, indeed, are the only commercial streets in the US that can compare with the immense length of East Colfax in Denver; the only parts of Los Angeles flat enough and boring enough to compare with the cities of the Middle West.

Yet this undistinguished townscape and its underlying flat topography were quite essential in producing the distinctively Angeleno ecologies that surround it on every side. In a sense it is a great service area feeding and supplying the foothills and beaches – across its flatness of instant track-laying ballast, the first five arms of the railroad system were spread with as little difficulty as toy trains on the living-room carpet, and later the Pacific Electric inter-urban lines, and later still the freeways. The very first railroad of all in the area, the Wilmington line, ran down across the plains to the harbour, but it was the Long Beach line of the Pacific Electric with its spurs to Redondo and San Pedro and its entanglements with the Los Angeles Pacific (which it bought out in 1906) which really began the great internal network that used the plains to link downtown, the foothills, and the beaches into a single comprehensible whole.

Watts was the very centre of all this action, a key junction and interchange between the long distance trunk routes, the inter-urbans and the street railways. It is doubtful if any part of Greater Los Angeles, even downtown, was so well connected to so many places – whatever local ecological disadvantages Watts may have suffered from its flatness and dryness, it was still a strategically well-placed community to live in. And with the beginning of the sixties, and the passing away of the last PE connexions, no place was more strategically ill-placed for anything, as the freeways with their different priorities threaded across the plains and left Watts always on one side. Whatever else has ailed Watts – and it is black on practically every map of disadvantages – its isolation from transportation contributes to every one of its misfortunes.

The difference in priorities of the original freeways is worth noting here, because those priorities have changed drastically since. The

Pasadena before the war, and the Hollywood immediately after, pursued affluence over the hills into the valleys beyond. They were strictly foothill affairs. But within a decade after the war's end, the flatlands were beginning to draw the network south, and by the mid sixties, the greatest mileage of freeways was in the plains, and beginning to bear an ever stronger resemblance to the original railroad network of the 1870s. And in those decades the plains began to impose their style on the freeways – instead of having to follow the landscape; they began to create the landscape. For miles across the flatlands the freeways are conspicuously the biggest human artefact, the only major disturbance of the land-surface, involving vastly more earth-moving than the railways did.

In areas like Palms, or Bell Gardens, or over between Willowbrook and Hawthorne, the banks and cuttings of the freeways are often the only topographical features of note in the townscape [86], and the

86. Townscape of freeway-land

planting on their slopes can make a contribution to the local environment that outweighs the disturbances caused by their construction – a view of a bank of artfully varied tree-planting can easily be a lot more rewarding than a prospect of endless flat backyards.

But the freeways are also beginning to have distinctive if oblique effects on the nature of the built environment too. Wherever a freeway crosses one of the more desirable residential areas of the plains – say, the San Diego south to a point just beyond International airport – it seems to produce a shift in land values that almost always leads to the construction of dingbats. This useful term – 'the basic Los Angeles Dingbat' – was probably invented by Francis Ventre during the year he taught at UCLA and lived in a prime example of the type within handy traffic-roaring distance of the San Diego, and denotes the current minimal form of multi-family residential unit.

It is normally a two storey walk-up apartment-block developed back over the full depth of the site [87a, b, c,], built of wood and stuccoed over. These are the materials that Rudolph Schindler and others used to build the first modern architecture in Los Angeles, and the dingbat, left to its own devices, often exhibits the basic characteristics of a primitive modern architecture. Round the back, away from the public gaze, they display simple rectangular forms and flush smooth surfaces, skinny steel columns and simple boxed balconies, and extensive overhangs to shelter four or five cars.

But out the front, dingbats cannot be left to their own devices; the front is a commercial pitch and a statement about the culture of individualism. A row of dingbats with standardized neat backs and sides will have every street façade competitively individual, to the extent that it is hard to believe that similar buildings lie behind. Everything that Nathanael West said, in *The Day of the Locust*, about the fanciful houses in Pinyon Canyon is true of the styles of the dingbats, except that they are harder to trace back to historical precedents, every style having been through the Los Angeles mincer. Everything is there from

Tacoburger Aztec to Wavy-line Moderne, from Cod Cape Cod to unsupported Jaoul vaults, from Gourmet Mansardic to Polynesian Gabled and even – in extremity – Modern Architecture.

The dingbat, even more than the occasional tower blocks below Hollywood or along Wilshire, is the true symptom of Los Angeles' urban Id trying to cope with the unprecedented appearance of residential densities too high to be subsumed within the illusions of homestead living. But these symptoms are still quite localized; across most of the basic plain, the Angeleno, his car and his house can still sprawl with the ease to which almost unlimited land has accustomed them. The dream, the illusion holds still, even if somewhere like Watts shows how slender is the hold of the illusion. But even there, just south of the cindered vacant lots and emergency installations on devastated 103rd Street, the visitor will come upon blocks of neat little houses in tidy gardens, proof that even there the plainsman's dream of urban homesteading can still be made real.

87a, b, c. Dingbat architecture of freeway-land

88. Barnsdall Lodge, Griffith Park, 1920,
R. M. Schindler, architect (for Frank Lloyd Wright)

9   Architecture III: The Exiles

A major modern architect in exile is almost automatically assumed to be a refugee from the Nazi persecutions of the early 1930s – the general history of modern architecture, written by refugees of that generation about other refugees of that generation, has still to face up to the consequences of the earlier exiles who gave Southern California an independent body of modern architecture contemporary with the rise of the International Style in Europe, or to acknowledge the fact that in Southern California some worthwhile possibilities of pre-1914 European architecture were to achieve a fulfilment denied them in Europe.

These exiles and possibilities reached the area by different routes and a variety of accidents. Kem Weber, one of the first, arrived in California early in 1914 to supervise work on the German Pavilion at the Panama Pacific exhibition, stayed on after the war broke out, and reached Los Angeles in 1921. His training and background in Bruno Paul's office in Berlin sets him apart slightly from the rest of the connexion, but he had contacted Rudolph Schindler soon after his arrival. Schindler, who trained under the great Otto Wagner at the Academy in Vienna, can be regarded as more typical (in so far as anyone is). He had gone to take a job in Chicago in 1914, visited the West the next year, committed himself to Frank Lloyd Wright in 1918 and went to California with him in 1920, where – in the first instance – he supervised the work on Wright's great houses of the Hollywood period, and designed the little lodge below the Barnsdall house [88] on Wright's behalf.

Schindler's personality and activities at this time seem to have been decisive in many ways, but it is difficult, now that more is known about the full range and depth of the student work in the *Wagner-schule* before the First World War [89], not to wonder how much the

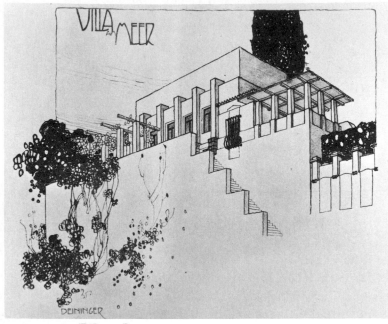

89. Project for hilltop villa, 1904,
Wagnerschule expertise by Wunibald Deininger

unique stylistic tendencies of those Wright houses may have been due
to his Viennese assistant on the spot. Wright had done hillside houses
before, but none attach themselves to a slope or ridge as these do, the
general air of fortification and enclosure about the Ennis house is
strikingly at variance with the general trend of his earlier designs, but
not altogether dissimilar to the defensive backside that Schindler's
own house turns towards the traffic on King's Road.

In Schindler's work these echoes of the *Wagnerschule* are persistent,
if just below the surface, but perhaps the most important thing he
brought out of Vienna was not a stylistic reminiscence at all, but the
creative personality of Richard Neutra. However, there was an im-

portant intermediate step in Neutra's case – Berlin, where he shared an office with Eric Mendelsohn, and this, as much as the half-generation difference in age (born 1887 and 1892 respectively) may go some way to account for the significant differences of architectural intention between the two. Plus differences in personality, of course – their joint office in King's Road did not last long, and probably would not have done even if no immediate cause of quarrel had arisen, but whatever one may feel about the rights and wrongs of that case, however one may rate their relative merits as architects, there can be no doubt that Neutra's has been the biggest architectural reputation in Los Angeles from 1930 almost to the present time.

And the Mendelsohn/Neutra connexion also seems to have been instrumental in bringing the ingenious and underrated talents of J. R. Davidson to Los Angeles, thus completing the dramatis personae for the rise of Angeleno Modern, which consisted of the names already mentioned – Wright, Schindler, Neutra, Weber, Davidson – and Jacques Peters, who did the interiors of Bullock's-Wilshire. These six took part together in a group exhibition in 1931; the catalogue angered Wright, Schindler was angered by Wright's attitude and their association was broken off. The result was to leave the Angeleno modernists even more cut off than before, in an isolation more profound than that of the Gill and Greene generation. However cut off California might have been before 1914 from world culture, that generation were at least still on the continent where they had been raised and trained, but the German-speaking contingent of the twenties were an ocean and a continent's width away from their native scenes, largely ignored by the rest of the US and effectively out of touch with the new architecture of the rest of the world. Neutra, however, did keep open a tenuous line of contact with Europe, but the flow of information was mostly eastwards – it gave Europe Neutra's *Wie baut Amerika* and secured the publication of Wright's Barnsdall house and Schindler's Howe residence in Bruno Taut's *Modern Architecture*.

So there they were, face to face with Southern California, afloat in its atmosphere of permissive extravagance, but with little cultural support except their original debts to Vienna and the *Wagnerschule* – it must have been this sense of an old indebtedness that prompted someone to serialize Otto Wagner's *Moderne Architektur* in the *Southwestern Builder and Contractor* from July 1938 onwards. Indebtedness it must have been; the exiles could hardly have needed reassurance by then, they were as well-established in Los Angeles as any modern architects could be anywhere in the world at that time, and they must have known that their security of place thereabouts was due to talent, and the support of one or two local enthusiasts for the new style.

Those supporting enthusiasts do not seem to have come – as is sometimes supposed – from German-speaking members of the film colony; a check of the names of their patrons in the twenties shows remarkably few German names, and the prime patron of the movement rejoiced in the thoroughly Anglo-Saxon name of Lovell. Not quite prime in the sense of chronology; Schindler had done a few small buildings before Philip Lovell came to him with the beach house commission, but it was that commission, and Lovell's later one to Neutra, that seems to have got their professional careers as independent architects properly under way.

Nevertheless, those earlier small works of Schindler's included the most remarkable design he was ever to produce – the house for himself and Clyde Chase [90a, b] on King's Road. Its system of interlocking garden-courts, flanked by living spaces that had open glass fronts and almost fortified backs made of tilted-up concrete slabs, is a model exercise in the interpenetration of indoor and outdoor spaces, a brilliant adaptation of simple constructional technology to local environmental needs and possibilities, and perhaps the most unobtrusively enjoyable domestic habitat ever created in Los Angeles. The design draws deeply on previous work in the area – the form of the concrete walls owes a clear debt to adobe building, their technology to Irving

90 a, b. Schindler/Chase house, King's Road, 1921,
R. M. Schindler, architect; *above*, under construction, and *below,* as it is now

Gill (whose Dodge house would have been visible from the site), but their combination and exploitation is genuinely original.

To my mind, he never did anything quite as good again, but it was the Lovell beach house at Newport [91] that formed the basis of his international reputation. Designed and built between 1923 and 1926,

91. Lovell beach house, Newport Beach, 1923–6, R. M. Schindler, architect

it was a world-class building not only because of its quality as a design, but also because its style, and manner of handling space, demand comparison with the best European work of the same period – and emerges from the comparison enhanced, not diminished. Put alongside, say, Le Corbusier's Villa Cook, its catalogued virtues reveal a building that could carry all Le Corbusier's theoretical propositions. It has a concrete frame which raises it clear of the ground on legs; it has a two-storey studio-type living-room and a roof terrace; it has parking space, a play area and a wash-up at ground-floor level. But the Corbu version is a timid, constrained design whose spatial adventures take place only within the almost unbroken cube of the building envelope, whereas Schindler's spatial extravagances break forward and oversail the ground floor, with staircases threaded visibly through the frame.

The differences are of social milieu and climate as much as of architectural temperament – what kind of architect might Corbu have become in Southern California? Could he have made any use of that sudden freedom that matured Schindler so early; alternatively, could he have broken out of the type-casting as a purely domestic architect that ultimately denied Schindler a chance to do any of the large-scale projects that were, surely, within the range of his talents. But apartment complexes were to be the largest schemes that Schindler would build, and they were not large; shops, restaurants, and a solitary church in Watts were to be his only buildings that could be called public.

However, his output in the domestic field was to be long and seemingly inexhaustible in its inventions, and – once he had mastered the local idiom of stucco over wood framing, in the Sachs apartments of 1928 – it appears to have had a sort of underground influence on common commercial building. The unadorned rear elevations of dingbats in Freewayland often have a Schindlerian air about their simple assembly of flat stuccoed planes – the talent that had nourished itself on elements of the Spanish Colonial Revival at the beginning of

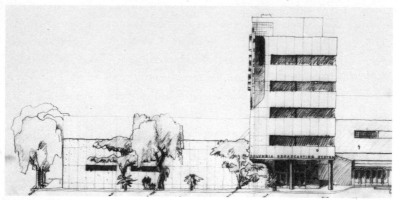

92. CBS Headquarters building (drawing), 1936, William Lescaze, architect

the twenties (as Gebhard suggests) also helped to sustain those elements into a much later age, as will be seen.

But in the middle years of his creative life, as the twenties became the thirties, he was, quite simply, the master of the International Style in Los Angeles. Though later historians have tended to speak as if that style only arrived in California with William Lescaze's CBS Building [92] of 1936, Schindler had been exploring its possibilities and pushing out its frontiers (for his own benefit, since the rest of the

93 (*opposite below*). Oliver house, Silverlake, 1933, R. M. Schindler, architect

94. Tischler house, Westwood, 1950, R. M. Schindler, architect

world knew almost nothing about him) with a confidence that borders on brio. The terraced Wolfe house on Catalina Island, together with the Oliver [93], Rodakiewicz, and Bush houses, constitute a body of work that need shame no architect in the world in those years, and by the time the CBS building arrived, Schindler had finished with the style the world called International and believed to be a post-war European invention, and had set out in search of a more complex use of space and a more liberated aesthetic – as in the Kallie studio of 1945 or the Tischler house [94] five years later, three years before his death.

Neutra's beginnings in Los Angeles were very much as an offshoot of Schindler's office, and the budding-off process was painful and left lasting wounds. The whole story cannot be told even now; though Neutra too is dead and safe from scandal, let it suffice here to say that Schindler had got as far with the project for the Lovell house in Griffith Park as to have made sketches and studied possible sites with the client – but Neutra got the job. It seems not to have been his first

independent design in Los Angeles, but it was the most important of the first and still forms the secure base of his reputation.

Yet the two Lovell commissions, almost more than any other buildings from their hands, underline the differences between Neutra and Schindler. The beach house is the work of an architect with the same kind of background as a Gropius or a Corbu, but Californiated – European architecture going with the flow of the California dream. The Griffith Park house [95a, b], by contrast, reveals Neutra as an architect using the Californian opportunity to make a European dream come true – the lightweight steel frame, the prefabricated panels, the suspended balconies, the conspicuously advanced mechanical specification, the edgy detailing, look like an attempt to realize a purely European vision of Machine Age architecture. It lacks the relaxation that makes Schindler's architecture as easy to take as any in Los Angeles, but it does have the nervous feeling of creative *angst* that makes European modern of the twenties appear heroically innovative.

95a, b. Health house,
Griffith Park, 1929,
Richard Neutra, architect

It has the air of an intellectual construction rather than a physical artefact, epitomized by that diagrammatically skinny detailing that was to be Neutra's trade mark for a decade or more.

Surprisingly, that skinny detailing does not appear significantly in the work of Kocher and Frey, who were working in Southern California from 1934, and had achieved an epitome of European concepts of economy applied to U S lightweight construction in their Aluminaire house in New York before coming West. Where it does reappear, however, is in early works by Thornton Abell [96] and Raphael Soriano, and this may be significant because Soriano is one of the few links between the exile generation and the bright young Americans (like Charles Eames) who built the steel and glass houses of the fifties – and such links between one style and the next are very rare in Los Angeles.

96. Abell house, Pacific Palisades, 1937, Thornton Abell, architect

But this is to get too far ahead of the Lovell house, which was completed in 1930. Neutra's creative career did not hit its full and honorific stride until 1933 or so. In that year he built his own house by Silverlake, and had a couple of public buildings in hand before the next two years were out: a school in Bell, and the California Military Academy. In 1938 began his involvement with apartment building on the Wolfskill rancho in Westlake: the Strathmore apartments [97], followed almost at once by the Kelton and Landfair blocks, and the Elkay a decade later. The Kelton also received an AIA honour award and for another fifteen years or so he averaged at least one such citation or award per annum.

There is a double import to these honours; they meant that the profession was catching up with Neutra, could understand his intentions enough to honour them – and to imitate them. He began to

97. Strathmore apartments, Westwood, 1938, Richard Neutra, architect

stand out less from the flock, so that one stumbles across average good buildings – the Eagle Rock club-house, Orange Coast College, Northwestern Mutual [98] – that one is surprised to find are the work of his office, rather than some good straight commercial design organization like the Victor Gruen office, which did Mid-Wilshire Medical Building [99]. But if the average run of architects was beginning to challenge him on larger commissions (there is something sadly

good-average about his work at San Fernando State College, or the Hall of Records) Neutra began in the fifties to design stunning houses once more. The more remarkable ones are peripheral to Los Angeles proper – like the extraordinary Moore house at Ojai – but

98 (*opposite*). Northwestern Mutual Insurance Offices, Los Angeles, 1950,
Richard Neutra, architect

99. Mid-Wilshire Medical Building, Los Angeles, 1950
Victor Gruen, architect

100. Hammerman house, Westwood, 1949, Richard Neutra, architect

in Palos Verdes, Westwood [100], Bel Air, Beverly Hills, and Pasadena, he built a sequence of (for him) pleasantly romantic houses. They are romantic in the sense that the detail is a little less skinny, and the use of materials much less diagrammatic – you feel he begins to value brick or steel for their character as substances, not just their performance – and the living spaces within are intimately involved with the out-doors. And in 1964 he rebuilt his own house after a fire, so much nearer to his own dreams and heart's desire that he was still talking about it a year later.

By then, however, he had achieved a notable 'first' in Internal Combustion City – a drive-in church. If there is a building that sums up, quietly and monumentally, what the peculiar automotive mania of

101. Garden Grove drive-in Church, 1962, Richard Neutra, architect

Los Angeles is all about, Garden Grove Community Church [101] must be the one – not least in the way so much of its detailing (canopies over some doors) and silhouette (ranked pylons against the sky) uncannily recall the characteristic detailing of such accepted monuments of Autopia as Five-Minute Car-Washes, or Ships coffee shop on Wilshire Boulevard [102]. Conscious imitation of what he must have regarded as a pseudo architecture beneath his attention seems out of the question – but the alternative is to credit such forms and usages with a subconscious archetypal value that is not usually accorded to the architecture of commercial fantasy.

Or, the connexion may be older and deeper but less magical – Schindler and Neutra had done so much to domesticate international

102. Ships Restaurant, Westwood Village, 1963,
Armet and Davis, architects

modern architecture in Los Angeles that they might, almost un-
consciously themselves, have put these forms into circulation and
imitation. In a less ornate connexion, the influence of their presence
and their example seems very clear; they helped to give architectural
legitimacy to the kind of building that economic necessity was tending
to extract from the Spanish Colonial Revival. If it is possible to put up
a simple stuccoed box in Los Angeles and regard the result as architecture, it is as much due to what the pioneer modernists have done as
it is to plain avarice stripping the Hispanic tradition of its ornamental
detail.

Very large areas of Los Angeles are made out of just these kind of
elementary cubes – they nestle among the foothills and line the
straight avenues of the plains. They are economically, structurally, and
– given the sunshine – architecturally, the local norm and vernacular.

103. Apartment blocks, Beverly Hills, c. 1960

Anyone who begins to understand Los Angeles visually has to accept, even celebrate, their normative standing – as David Hockney has done in his paintings of the city. Furthermore, the plain plastered cube has the added status now of forming a firm vernacular basis from which more conscious architecture can develop. By this I don't mean just the fancy fronts of the otherwise plain dingbats, or their more pretentious multi-storey cousins [103] in the apartment-zoned areas of Beverly Hills, but also something simpler and more notably architectural.

For instance, the studio-house on Melrose Avenue that Frank Gehry built for Lou Danziger in 1968 [104]. Melrose is just the kind of street that forms the natural habitat for commercial stuccoed cubes, and the studio is built in exactly that same way – wood frame with a rendered surface, though the stucco is heavily rough-cast to provide a surface that can absorb the dirt of a heavily used thoroughfare without becoming streaky. But although the forms look commonly boxy, the planning and organization are not. Instead they recall the design of studio houses in Europe in the twenties – Gehry admits to having lived for a time in Meudon, but not to any influence from, say, the van Doesburg house there. Yet he has even put a two-storey studio window . at the back with doors in the lower part, very much in the Parisian mode. But if there are any purely stylistic pretensions they are of a much later vintage – the two pop-up skylights over the domestic wing clearly belong to the age of Charles Moore, though only in intentions, not in their forms. But these are marginal matters; what is important and striking is the way in which this elegantly simple envelope not only reaffirms the continuing validity of the stucco box as Angeleno architecture, but does so in a manner that can stand up to international scrutiny. The cycle initiated by Schindler comes round again with deft authority.

104. Danziger Studio, Southern Hollywood, 1968, Frank Gehry, architect

10 A Note on Downtown ...

... because that is all downtown Los Angeles deserves. This opinion will undoubtedly offend entrenched downtown interests, and historians who still feel that the development of the city must, in some way, follow consequentially from the foundation of the pueblo on a site somewhere on the northern fringe of the present downtown area. There is clearly a feeling that' downtown has got to be important because downtowns are significant and important places in all self-respecting cities, and there have been seriously-intended and massively-funded attempts to reactivate the area; hence the cultural 'Acropolis' being created on Bunker Hill above City Hall, and hence also the cluster of new commercial towers around the area loosely referred to as 'Broadway and Seventh'. But quite typically, one of the most prestigious new cultural institutions, the County Art Museum, is seven miles away on the rival downtown of Wilshire Boulevard, and it is difficult in terms of the general style of the metropolis at large not to feel that this is a much more appropriate setting than that of the concert hall and theatre on Bunker Hill.

Pueblo-centric historians, of course, have always tended to see the development of the city as a 'normal' outward sprawl from a centre which is older than the rest of the city, but in spite of the chronological priority of the pueblo, other areas in the plains, foothills and coast had begun to develop before the pueblo could mutate convincingly into an authoritative downtown. This is not to propose that the pueblo did not become the focus of the transportation net from which the whole area was opened up, nor that it was this settlement that gave its name to the completed Southern California metropolis, but its relationship to the other parts of the metropolis never carried the sense of moral and municipal hegemony that normally

1850, population 2,500 1893, population 160,000

105. Urban growth in the Greater Los Angeles area, 1850–1933

exists between a central city and its satellite suburbs. Anaheim was already big enough to get itself built into the original railroad deal with the Southern Pacific in 1873, and the stand-offish independence of Pasadena has become proverbial. To judge from the population statistics [105], the centre most nearly outbalanced its supposed satellites in about 1910 when the legal City had some three hundred thousand of

1915–16, population 1,000,000   1932–3, population 3,500,000

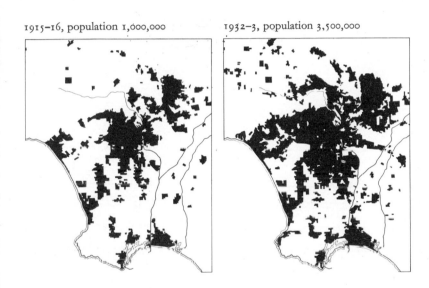

the county's half million inhabitants, but its boundaries had already been extended beyond even the original pueblo's capacious four square leagues of land, and the annexation of the San Fernando Valley in 1915 makes any further calculation of this sort nonsensical. In any case, the growth of the metropolis in the era of the Pacific Electric inter-urban railway makes visible and final nonsense of any idea of regular centrifugal growth. To speak of 'sprawl' in the sense that, say, Boston, Mass., sprawled centrifugally in its street-railway years, is to ignore the observable facts.

And those observable facts, in the downtown area, seem neither very attractive nor historically rewarding [106]. Even the site of the original pueblo's plaza, as reconstructed in the well-known but under-criticized map in Bancroft's *History*, is now lost, was already lost at the time of Lieutenant Ord's original survey of the city in 1849, and thus leaves a mystery at the very heart of the city. The problem is that the location of the Plaza church [107] rules out both the present plaza and the Olvera street complex as possible sites for the plaza shown in Bancroft, which has the site for the church in the south-east

106 (*opposite*). Air-view of central downtown area, Los Angeles

107. Plaza church and Pico block in 1968

corner of the plaza, whereas the church is now at the south-western corner of the Olvera Street complex, or the north-western of the present Plaza.

There is also the problem of orientation to bedevil any attempted reconstruction. Bancroft doubtless took the orientation of the plaza on his map from the alignment of the streets as Ord found them at the time of his survey, which was about thirty-eight degrees off the normal orientation, by the cardinal compass points. Yet Governor de Neve's original instruments creating the pueblo had ordained streets running

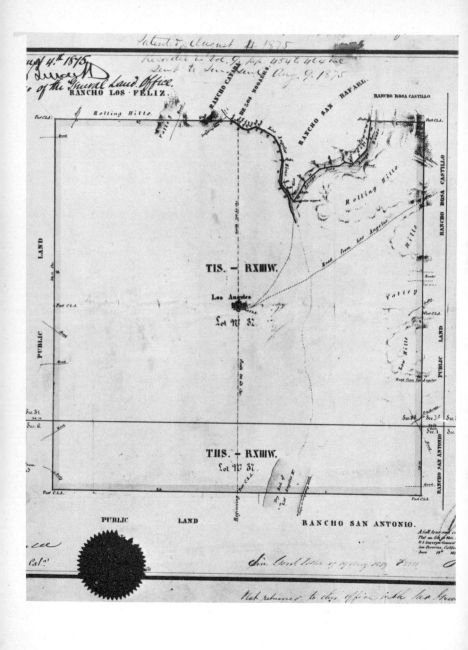

north-south and east-west, and the four square leagues of land belonging to the pueblo, as confirmed in US law, also had the true cardinal orientation [108]. It begins to look as if there is substance in the supposition that the original pueblo settlement was moved and reconstituted, hurriedly and more than once, as a result of floods or earthquakes, in its earlier days, and that the cardinal orientation was lost through inadvertence, or altered to make more realistic use of the land nearer to the hills.

It is clear that as late as Ruxton's survey of 1873 (which, like Ord's, was also a primitive town plan) there were numerous buildings that corresponded neither to the survey's building-lines nor to any kind of comprehensible orientation or street plan; as if the townsite had become completely higgledy-piggledy, and had been for some several decades, as is suggested by the Mexican ordinance of 1836 to regularize the pueblo and its buildings. So, disoriented and displaced, the present-day visitor to the presumed heart of the original city finds himself unable to relate meaningfully to the buildings and land he can see. Here, in the only area that has the kind of multi-layered history usual in older cities, it is less immediately comprehensible than in the newer areas that visiting planners affect to find incomprehensible.

On a straightforward catalogue of representative monuments, downtown does sound like a true urban centre; it has City Hall and law courts, the Union Station, the Cathedral of Santa Vibiana, it has the oldest brick structure in the city, and the Plaza church and the old Plaza firehouse and such esteemed monuments of commerce as the Pico block, now over a century old, and the Bradbury Building whose central well of cast-iron balconies, stairs, and open elevators [109] makes it one of the most magnificent relics of nineteenth-century commercial architecture anywhere in the world. But like everything

108. Pueblo lands as surveyed by Henry Hancock, 1858

else in downtown it stands as an unintegrated fragment in a downtown
scene that began to disintegrate long ago – out of sheer irrelevance as
far as one can see. Many US cities have had their downtown areas fall
into this kind of desuetude, and have made equally irrelevant attempts to
revitalize them (Minneapolis is the example I know best) but in none of
the others does one have quite such a strong feeling that this is where
the action cannot possibly be.

Many well-established Angelenos audibly and frequently regret
the fact that most of downtown is now little more than a badly planned
and badly run suburban shopping centre for those who cannot
afford cars to get to the real 'suburbs', rather than the vital heart of a
thriving urban community, but I think that even they are trying to
force the city into categories of judgement that simply do not apply.
It would be nice if Pershing Square was still full of old men playing
chess (or whatever it was) and if the Angel's Flight funicular still
climbed between those narrow streets of picturesquely crumbling
rooming-houses, but it could only happen nowadays under some such
auspices as produced Olvera Street – or Disneyland!

In terms of the real life of the seventy-mile-square metropolis
today, most of what is contained within the rough central parallelo-
gram of the Santa Monica, Harbor, Santa Ana, and San Bernardino
freeways could disappear overnight and the bulk of the citizenry
would never even notice. It must be this sense of irrelevance that
undermines any feeling of conviction in the architecture of the new
buildings that have been put up there recently for commercial or

110a. Downtown: the Hall of Records, right, and the tower of City Hall

civic purposes. They are, frankly, a gutless-looking collection [110a], but not gracious with it; they are neither tough-minded nor sensitive, nor architectural monuments, nor Pop extravaganzas. Nor need this judgement be much amended in favour of the new crop of seventies skyscrapers that have appeared in the south-western quarter of down-town since this book first appeared [110b]. However handsome they may be in their standard livery of dark glass and steel, however ingenious and hopefully civic-minded the pedestrian shopping malls that burrow among their foundations, they are simply illusions in a city of illusions.

The illusion, quite simply, is that Los Angeles now has a downtown, and the illusion works, briefly, because one recognizes a cluster of dark glass towers nowadays as meaning 'downtown' wherever it appears . . . and there's the rub, because it appears all over the United States and elsewhere, and all that Los Angeles has acquired is the air of having a downtown like all the others. Or, if you insist on a purely Angeleno justification for this short dozen of towers, then it can only be as yet another ghetto, this time a financial one, complete with the huddled paranoias that go with such defensive enclaves. Already the promoters of these developments are claiming that they will 'hold back the tide of urban blight along the line of Spring Street' – a static and monumentalizing view of urban development, underwritten by

110b. Downtown: new office towers from the north-west

frightened money from the East that will never know how to go with the flow of Angeleno life.

Those who do go with the flow, the motorized citizens rolling at night along the four freeways that box in the central downtown cavity, can at least look at the city of illusion created by the lights of the buildings. But they are more likely to notice the light (in the singular) of that very singular building, the gleaming cube of the Water and Power offices. It is the kind of monument that architects can relevantly offer to this city founded precisely on water and power – and transportation, which has monumentalized itself in the freeways themselves, and really needs no further monument, since they serve and facilitate that unfocused ubiquity that has made Los Angeles what it is – and has shrivelled the heart out of downtown.

11 Ecology IV: Autopia

The first time I saw it happen nothing registered on my conscious mind, because it all seemed so natural – as the car in front turned down the off-ramp of the San Diego freeway, the girl beside the driver pulled down the sun-visor and used the mirror on the back of it to tidy her hair. Only when I had seen a couple more incidents of the kind did I catch their import: that coming off the freeway is coming in from outdoors. A domestic or sociable journey in Los Angeles does not end so much at the door of one's destination as at the off-ramp of the freeway, the mile or two of ground-level streets counts as no more than the front drive of the house.

In part, this is a comment on the sheer vastness of the movement pattern of Los Angeles, but more than that it is an acknowledgement that the freeway system in its totality is now a single comprehensible place, a coherent state of mind, a complete way of life, the fourth ecology of the Angeleno. Though the famous story in *Cry California* magazine about the family who actually lived in a mobile home on the freeways is now known to be a jesting fabrication, the idea was

111. Freeway-scape, drivers' eye view

immediately convincing (several other magazines took it seriously and wanted to reprint it) because there was a great psychological truth spoken in the jest. The freeway is where the Angelenos live a large part of their lives [111].

Such daily sacrifices on the altar of transportation are the common lot of all metropolitan citizens of course. Some, with luck, will spend less time on the average at these devotions, and many will spend them under far more squalid conditions (on the Southern Region of British Railways, or in the New York subway, for instance) but only Los Angeles has made a mystique of such proportions out of its commuting technology that the whole world seems to know about it – tourist postcards from London do not show Piccadilly Circus underground station, but cards from Los Angeles frequently show local equivalents like the 'stack' intersection in downtown; Paris is not famous as the home of the Metro in the way Los Angeles is famous as the home of the Freeway (which must be galling for both Detroit and New York which have better claims, historically). There seem to be two major reasons for their dominance in the city image of Los Angeles and both are aspects of their inescapability; firstly, that they are so vast that you cannot help seeing them, and secondly, that there appears no alternative means of movement and you cannot help using them. There are other and useful streets, and the major boulevards provide an excellent secondary network in many parts of the city, but psychologically, all are felt to be tributary to the freeways.

Furthermore, the actual experience of driving on the freeways prints itself deeply on the conscious mind and unthinking reflexes. As you acquire the special skills involved, the Los Angeles freeways become a special way of being alive, which can be duplicated, in part, on other systems (England would be a much safer place if those skills could be inculcated on our motorways) but not with this totality and extremity. If motorway driving anywhere calls for a high level of attentiveness, the extreme concentration required in Los Angeles seems to bring on a state of heightened awareness that some locals find mystical.

That concentration is required beyond doubt, for the freeways can kill – hardly a week passed but I found myself driving slowly under police control past the wreckage of at least one major crash. But on the other hand the freeways are visibly safe – I never saw any of these incidents, or even minor ones, actually happening, even in weeks where I found I had logged a thousand miles of rush-hour driving. So one learns to proceed with a strange and exhilarating mixture of long-range confidence and close-range wariness. And the freeway system can fail; traffic jams can pile up miles long in rush-hours or even on sunny Sunday afternoons, but these jams are rarely stationary for as long as European expectations would suggest. Really serious jams seem to be about as frequent as hold-ups on London suburban railways, and might – if bad – disrupt the working day of about the same number of citizens, but for most of the time traffic rolls comfortably and driving conditions are not unpleasant. As one habituated to the psychotic driving (as Gerald Priestland has called it) in English cities, and the squalor of the driving conditions, I cannot find it in me to complain about the freeways in Los Angeles; they work uncommonly well.

Angelenos, who have never known anything worse than their local system, find plenty to complain about, and their conversations are peppered with phrases like 'being stuck in a jam in the October heat with the kids in the back puking with the smog'. At first the visitor takes these remarks seriously; they confirm his own most deeply ingrained prejudices about the city that has 'sold its soul to the motor car'. Later, I came to realize that they were little more than standard rhetorical tropes, like English complaints about the weather, with as little foundation in the direct personal experience of the speakers.

This is not to minimize the jams, or even the smog, but both need to be seen in the context of comparisons with other metropolitan areas. On what is regarded as a normally clear day in London, one cannot see as far through the atmosphere as on some officially smoggy days I have experienced in Los Angeles. Furthermore, the photochemical irritants in the smog (caused by the action of sunlight on nitrogen oxides) can be extremely unpleasant indeed in high concentrations, but for the concentration to be high enough to make the corners of my eyes itch painfully is rare in my personal experience, and at no time does the smog contain levels of soot, grit, and corroding sulphur compounds that are still common in the atmospheres of older American and European cities.

It is the psychological impact of smog that matters in Los Angeles. The communal trauma of Black Wednesday (8 September 1943), when the first great smog zapped the city in solid, has left permanent scars, because it broke the legend of the land of eternal sunshine. It was only a legend; the area was never totally pure of atmosphere. The Spaniards called it the Bay of Smokes and could identify it from the ocean by the persistence of smoke from Indian camp-fires, while plots of land in South Cucamonga were advertised in the eighties as being free from 'fog-laden sea-breezes'. But there is a profound psychological difference between fogs caused by Nature's land-forms and light breezes and God-given water, and air-pollution due to the works of man. To make matters worse, analysis showed that a large part of the smog (though not all, one must emphasize) is due to effluents from the automobile. Angelenos were shocked to discover that it was their favourite toy that was fouling up their greatest asset.

But, psychologically shocked or no, most Angeleno freeway-pilots are neither retching with smog nor stuck in a jam; their white-wall tyres are singing over the diamond-cut anti-skid grooves in the concrete road surface, the selector-levers of their automatic gearboxes are firmly in *Drive*, and the radio is on. And more important than any of this, they are acting out one of the most spectacular paradoxes in the great debate between private freedom and public disipline that pervades every affluent, mechanized urban society.

The private car and the public freeway together provide an ideal – not to say idealized – version of democratic urban transportation: door-to-door movement on demand at high average speeds over a very large area. The degree of freedom and convenience thus offered to all but a small (but now conspicuous) segment of the population is such that no Angeleno will be in a hurry to sacrifice it for the higher efficiency but drastically lowered convenience and freedom of choice of any high-density public rapid-transit system. Yet what seems to be hardly noticed or commented on is that the price of rapid door-to-door transport on demand is the almost total surrender of personal freedom for most of the journey.

The watchful tolerance and almost impeccable lane discipline of Angeleno drivers on the freeways is often noted, but not the fact that both are symptoms of something deeper – willing acquiescence in an incredibly demanding man / machine system. The fact that no single ordinance, specification or instruction manual describes the system in its totality does not make it any less complete or all-embracing – or any less demanding. It demands, first of all, an open but decisive attitude to the placing of the car on the road-surface, a constant stream of decisions that it would be fashionable to describe as 'existential' or even 'situational', but would be better to regard simply as a higher form of pragmatism. The carriage-way is not divided by the kind of kindergarten rule of the road that obtains on British motorways, with their fast, slow, and overtaking lanes (where there are three lanes to use!). The three, four, or five lanes of an Angeleno freeway are virtually equal, the driver is required to select or change lanes according to his speed, surrounding circumstances and future intentions. If everybody does this with the approved mixture of enlightened self-interest and public spirit, it is possible to keep a very large flow of traffic moving quite surprisingly fast.

But at certain points, notably intersections, the lanes are not all equal – some may be pre-empted for a particular exit or change-over

ramp as much as a mile before the actual junction. As far as possible the driver must get set up for these pre-empted lanes well in advance, to be sure he is in them in good time because the topology of the intersections is unforgiving. Of course there are occasional clods and strangers who do not sense the urgency of the obligation to set up the lane required good and early, but fortunately they are only occasional (you soon get the message!), otherwise the whole system would snarl up irretrievably. But if these preparations are only an unwritten moral obligation, your actual presence in the correct lane at the inter-section is mandatory – the huge signs straddling the freeway to indicate the correct lanes must be obeyed because they are infallible.

At first, these signs can be the most psychologically unsettling of all aspects of the freeway – it seems incredibly bizarre when a sign directs one into the far left lane for an objective clearly visible on the right of the carriageway, but the sign must be believed. No human eye at windscreen level can unravel the complexities of even a relatively simple intersection [112] (none of those in Los Angeles is a symmetrical cloverleaf) fast enough for a normal human brain moving forward at up to sixty mph to make the right decision in time, and there is no alternative to complete surrender of will to the instructions on the signs.

But no permanent system of fixed signs can give warning of transient situations requiring decisions, such as accidents, landslips or other blockages. It is in the nature of a freeway accident that it involves a large number of vehicles, and blocks the carriageway so completely that even emergency vehicles have difficulty in getting to the seat of the trouble, and remedial action such as warnings and diversions may have to be phased back miles before the accident, and are likely to affect traffic moving in the opposite direction in the other carriageway as well. So, inevitably the driver has to rely on other sources of rapid information, and keeps his car radio turned on for warnings of delays and recommended diversions.

Now, the source of these radio messages is not a publicly-operated traffic-control radio-transmitter; they are a public service performed by the normal entertainment stations, who derive the information from the police, the Highway Patrol, and their own 'Sigalert' helicopter patrols. Although these channels of information are not provided as a designed component of the freeway system, but arise as an accidental by-product of commercial competition, they are no less essential to the system's proper operation, especially at rush hours. Thus a variety of commanding authorities – moral, governmental, commercial, and mechanical (since most drivers have surrendered control of the transmission to an automatic gearbox) – direct the freeway driver through a situation so closely controlled that, as has been judiciously observed on a number of occasions, he will hardly notice any difference when the freeways are finally fitted with computerized automatic control systems that will take charge of the car at the on-ramp and direct it at properly regulated speeds and correctly selected routes to a pre-programmed choice of off-ramp.

But it seems possible that, given a body of drivers already so well trained, disciplined, and conditioned, realistic cost-benefit analysis might show that the marginal gains in efficiency through automation might be offset by the psychological deprivations caused by destroying the residual illusions of free decision and driving skill surviving in the present situation. However inefficiently organized, the million or so human minds at large on the freeway system at any time comprise a far greater computing capacity than could be built into any machine currently conceivable – why not put that capacity to work by fostering the illusion that it is in charge of the situation?

If illusion plays as large a part in the working of the freeways as it does in other parts of the Angeleno ecology, it is not to be deprecated. The system works as well as it does because the Angelenos believe in it as much as they do; they may squeal when the illusion is temporarily shattered or frustrated; they may share the distrust of the

Division of Highways that many liberal souls currently (and under-standably) seem to feel; but on leaving the house they still turn the nose of the car towards the nearest freeway ramp because they still believe the freeways are the way to get there. They subscribe, if only covertly, to a deep-seated mystique of freeway driving, and I often suspect that the scarifying stories of the horrors of the freeways are deliberately put about to warn off strangers.

Partly this would be to keep inexperienced and therefore dangerous hayseeds off the carriageways, but it would also be to prevent the profanation of their most sacred ritual by the uninitiated. For the Freeway, quite as much as the Beach, is where the Angeleno is most himself, most integrally identified with his great city.

Say, isn't that your old Aunt Nabby who just passed you in the outer lane of the Berdoo at eighty? There she is, six months in Southern California and already she's got the glued up ash-blond hair, the wrap-around shades and the tight pants and . . . a chrome yellow Volkswagen with reversed wheels and a voom-voom exhaust.

Thus wrote Brock Yates in *Car and Driver* magazine, a capsule account of identification with Southern California citizenship via the auto-mobile as a work of art and the freeway as a suitable gallery in which to display it.

The automobile as art-work is almost as specific to the Los Angeles freeways as is the surf-board to the Los Angeles beaches. It has a lengthy tradition behind it, but that tradition drives far less from the imported dream cars, the mile-long Hispanos or the gold Dual-Ghias of the film stars, than from the wonders wrought in backyards by high-school drop-outs upon domestic Detroit-built machines. The art of customizing, of turning common family sedans into wild extrava-ganzas of richly coloured and exotically shaped metal, was delinquent in its origins, however much the present apologists of the hot-rod cult may try to pretend to the contrary, and the drag-racing which is almost the dominant local land-borne sport in Los Angeles is simply a

ritualized version of the illegal sprint races that used to take place on
the public highways.

But in the uninhibited inventiveness of master customizers like
George Barris [113] and Ed Roth, normal straight Los Angeles
found something that sprang from the dusty grass roots of its native
culture – 'to ride forth seeking romance . . . to speak in superlatives

113. Customized car, George Barris, designer

. . . to throw dignity out of the window, to dress dramatically . . . to
tackle the impossible' – tamed it, institutionalized it, and applied it in
some form to almost every vehicle awheel in the City of Angels
(whence its influence has spread back to Detroit and thus to all other
motorized parts of the globe). The customized automobile is the natural
crowning artefact of the way of life, the human ecology, it adorns.

If you regard the freeways, with Brock Yates, as an 'existential
limbo where man sets out each day in search of western-style individualism' then the assertiveness of the style of the art-automobile might be
regarded as an aid in that anxious search. But my own observations of
Angeleno drivers at close range suggests that many of those who
flaunt a wild rail on the Berdoo or the San Mo are relaxed and well-
adjusted characters without an identity problem in the world, for whom
the freeway is not a limbo of existential *angst*, but the place where they
spend the two calmest and most rewarding hours of their daily lives.

12 Architecture IV:
The Style That Nearly . . .

My first consciousness of any specific architecture in Los Angeles occurred almost exactly twenty years before writing these words (and probably triggered the process which led to them being written) when I discovered Charles Eames's house [114] in an American magazine. That experience was not unique; the Eames house has had a profound effect on many of the architects of my generation in Britain and Europe. It became the most frequently mentioned point of pilgrimage for intending visitors to Los Angeles among my friends, some of whom were later to edit a special issue of the English magazine *Architectural Design* devoted to Eames's work, and to his house. For most of two decades it has shared with Rodia's towers in Watts the distinction of being the best known and most illustrated building in Los Angeles (a fact which still surprises many Angelenos).

The reasons for the reputation of the Eames's house are as multi-farious as they always must be for a durable masterpiece. The inherent originality and quality of the design are manifest, but it is quite likely that the simultaneous appearance in the world's press of Eames's globally successful steel and moulded plywood chair, the most compelling artefact of its generation in some ways, helped to focus world attention on everything that Eames was doing at the time. Again, the style of both the house and the chair answered exactly to an emerging taste for that kind of fine-drawn design in many parts of the world. But the most crucial factor is external to Eames's qualities as a designer: it was the publication of the house, like the chair, in John Entenza's Los Angeles-based magazine *Arts and Architecture*.

114. Eames house, Pacific Palisades, 1949, Charles Eames, architect

Through the magazine, Entenza (who was not a native Angeleno, any more than Eames was) had promoted the Case Study Program of experimental houses, which included designs by most of the major design talents working in the modern idiom in the city – Neutra and Davidson, for instance, of the older generation; Soriano [115] of the middle group to which Eames really belongs also, since his house was the bridge to the fully-developed steel and glass style of the younger generation of Ellwood and Koenig. The Program, the magazine, Entenza, and a handful of architects really made it appear that Los Angeles was about to contribute to the world not merely odd works of architectural genius but a whole consistent style.

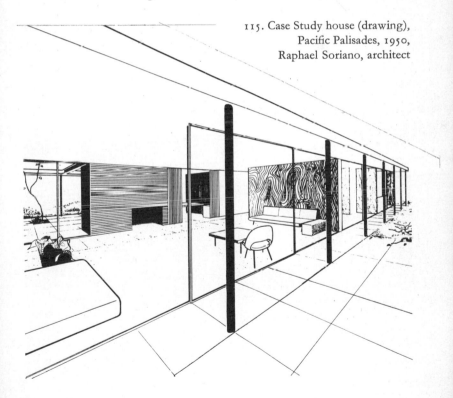

115. Case Study house (drawing),
Pacific Palisades, 1950,
Raphael Soriano, architect

Since that style was of glass carried in frames of visible steel, it was not utterly unique in its time; Mies van der Rohe's Farnsworth house and Philip Johnson's own glass pavilion are effectively contemporary with the beginning of the steel and glass phase of the Case Study Program, and the row of steel and glass houses by Korsmo and Norberg-Schulz outside Oslo had been built before the Program was finished. There has always been some discussion of the indebtedness of the Case Study style to Mies but there is little sign of it (except in the work of Ellwood) and the basic idea of houses as skinny steel frames infilled with glass has a tenuous local ancestry traceable back through Soriano – or so local sentiment loyally insists – and thus, presumably, to Neutra.

Whatever the sources, a style emerges almost unanimously and simultaneously in three houses completed in 1949–50: the Eames house, of course, Soriano's Case Study house, and – outside the Program – Ellwood's Hale house [116]. In all of these the steel is

116. Hale house, Beverly Hills, 1951, Craig Ellwood, architect

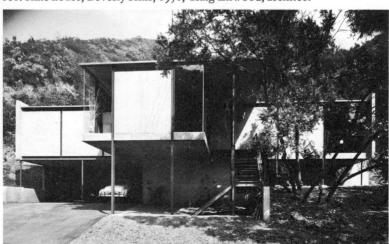

used in a very unmonumental manner, as compared with Mies's and Johnson's work back East. The metal sections are inclined to be skinny and they are not treated as being of any great visual consequence in themselves. In the Eames house the structural members had been fabricated originally for a different design, and had to be readapted, while the glazing was carried in off-the-peg standard window-frames ordered from the Truscon catalogue. In Soriano's design the steel uprights are plain tubes with their upper ends cross-slotted to accept fish-plates that were welded in to carry the ends of the horizontal members. Neither the cutting of the slots nor the weld-laying is anything beyond normal steel-assembly techniques, adequate to the building codes.

A similar attitude to detailing can be seen in much of Pierre Koenig's work inside and outside the Program. The welds are sufficient to their allotted tasks, and within the normal compass of the welder's craft. Compared with the fine-art weld-laying and subsequent grinding off with emery wheels at the Farnsworth house, this kind of work reveals again the absence of that heroic-style creative *angst* of the European-based modern movement, and gives an improvisatory air to the whole fabric. I have personally seen Koenig discussing on site some alterations to an existing house, confirming with the builder the way a sill-detail should be resolved, without any prepared drawings for guidance, but a great deal of trust in the craftsman's judgement – and craft.

If such details seem underdesigned, even careless in European eyes at first, there is nothing unconsidered about their exact location, which is the most calculated and critical part of the whole design. In the domestic work of both Ellwood and Koenig [117, 118], details of any sort are sparsely distributed, because structural joints are postponed as late as feasible along the horizontal plane; that is, spans are long and upright supports as rare as they can only be when using steel in light-weight single-storey construction. This is, *par excellence*, an architecture

117 (*opposite*). Case Study house 21, Wonderland Park, 1958,
Pierre Koenig, architect

118. Case Study house 22, Hollywood Hills, 1959, Pierre Koenig, architect

of elegant omission that takes Mies van der Rohe's dictum about *Weniger ist Mehr* even further than the Master himself had ever done.

Yet the very puritanism and understatement that we admire in the Case Study style make it an unlikely starter in the cultural ambience of Los Angeles – or rather, make it an unlikely finisher. The permissive atmosphere means that almost anything can be started; what one doubts is that there was enough flesh on these elegant bones to satisfy local tastes for long. Obviously the combination of transparent walls and solid roof answers well enough to Angeleno uncertainties about indoors and out, but the frankness with which the penetrable environment has been made visible [119] goes well beyond what seem to be the local norms, which were set, after all, by romantic masterpieces like the Gamble house, and confirmed by two subsequent generations of artful contrivance, ancient and modern, Nordic or Hispanic. Largely a product of Entenza's enthusiasms and constant exposure in *Arts and*

119. South Bay Bank, Manhattan Beach, 1956, Craig Ellwood, architect

Architecture, the style did not seem likely to survive, as a style, after Entenza left Los Angeles at the end of the fifties. By the time I first arrived in Los Angeles, I was told that the steel and glass architects were in dire straits generally, and that neither Koenig nor Ellwood had any new work in their offices.

The news was false almost as it was being uttered, as it turned out, but in the early sixties it was clear that the steel and glass style of domestic architecture we were visiting Los Angeles to see was no longer an active style, and nothing has emerged since then that adds up to an equally convincing style for modern housing. But the Case Study approach has had a fresh lease of life in the guise of a new stylish type of industrial architecture. Whereas the kind of architecture favoured by most Southern California aerospace and advanced technology companies has been both uninspired and uninspiring, one or two have worked with a style of architecture as new and keen as their techno-

120. Xerox Data Systems offices, El Segundo, 1966, Craig Ellwood, architect

logical insights. The news I had heard about Ellwood was falsified by the first commission for new buildings of his design for a company called Scientific Data Systems (later Xerox Data Systems), which has now resulted in a handsome sequence of industrial buildings [120] at El Segundo with – as is usual with Ellwood – detailing that is far less simple than appears at first sight.

If Ellwood and xds were alone in this, the survival of the style might be brushed off as no more than freak, a personal whimsy. The reason for taking its survival seriously is that another advanced technology company – Teledyne Systems – and another architect – Cesar Pelli – have opted for a similar style at Teledyne's [121] new plant at Northridge in the San Fernando Valley. Pelli, an Argentinian and one of the city's more interesting recent imports among archi-

121. Teledyne Systems, Northridge, 1968,
Cesar Pelli (for Daniel, Mann, Johnson & Meldenhall, architects)

tects, has not shown himself so far to be a man of particularly firm stylistic preferences and, like his teacher Eero Saarinen, has tended to use a 'style for the job'. The Teledyne plant (designed while he was with the Daniel, Mann, Johnson and Meldenhall office) therefore appears to represent a style selected as appropriate to the needs and character of the client's business.

What is striking is that, as a one-shot style adopted for a particular job, Pelli's version cleaves closer to the original manner of the Case Study style than Ellwood's now does. Ellwood's style has gone on developing organically, getting more and more extraordinarily skinny and idiosyncratic, with Miesian concepts like cruciform columns and exposed trusses shrunk by a factor of two, so that you have to wonder how so little steel can support so much roof. In the present state of the 'self-image' of systems technology there seems to be a certain appropriateness in this sparse and calculated style, but it remains to be seen if two plant-complexes constitute enough corpus of work and stylistic momentum to see the revived Case Study style through any economic or psychological recessions that may lie ahead. But, for me, at least, it is reassuring to see it flourishing again; the 'style that nearly didn't' might still surprise us all.

13 An Ecology for Architecture

An even greater urban vision than the view of Los Angeles from Griffith Park Observatory is the view of Los Angeles on a clear day from a high-flying aircraft. Within its vast extent can be seen its diverse ecologies of sea-coast, plain, and hill; within that diversity can be seen the mechanisms, natural and human, that have made those ecologies support a way of life – in the dry brown hills the flood-control basins brimming with ugly yellow water, the geometries of the orange-groves and vineyards, the bustling topologies of the freeway inter-sections, a splatter of light reflected from a hundred domestic swimming pools, the power of zoning drawn as a three-dimensional graph by the double file of towers and slabs along Wilshire Boulevard, the interlaced rails and roads in the Cajon and Soledad passes, the eastern and western gates of the city.

Overflying such a spectacle, it is difficult to doubt that it is a subject worthy of description, yet at ground level there have been many who were ready to cast doubt on the worth of such an enterprise. At one extreme, the distinguished Italian architect and his wife who, on discovering that I was writing this book, doubted that anyone who cared for architecture could lower himself to such a project and walked away without a word further. At the other extreme, two hippie girls who panhandled me for the mandatory dime outside *Color Me Aardvaark*, asked me why I had a camera round my neck and then riposted with 'Aw heck, there's lotsa picture-books about LA already!'

Between such unthinking hostility from outsiders, and equally unthinking indifference from the Angeleno equivalent of Cockneys, Los Angeles does not get the attention it deserves – it gets attention, but it's like the attention that Sodom and Gomorrah have received, primarily a reflection of other peoples' bad consciences. As a result of such failures of attention (Peter Hall ómitted it from his *World Cities*, in spite of his known enthusiasm for Los Angeles) puzzled outsiders, like the editor of *Progressive Architecture*, who would genuinely like to know more, are apt to suppose that the essence of Los Angeles must be curiously ineffable to anyone but its inhabitants.

Yet the city is as far from being an impenetrable mystery as it is from being an urbanistic disaster-area. From the time of Anton Wagner's exhaustive *Los Angeles . . . Zweimillionenstadt in Südkalifornien* of 1935, Los Angeles has supported an extensive and responsible literature of explication, and an equally extensive literature of well-informed abuse. And in view of the rather short history of construction and administration to be explained or abused, that literature ought by now to have made the place one of the most open books in the history of city-making.

On the other hand, there are many who do not wish to read the book, and would like to prevent others from doing so; they have soundly-based fears about what might happen if the secrets of the Southern Californian metropolis were too profanely opened and made plain. Los Angeles threatens the intellectual repose and professional livelihood of many architects, artists, planners, and environmentalists because it breaks the rules of urban design that they promulgate in works and writings and teach to their students. In so far as Los Angeles performs the functions of a great city, in terms of size, cosmopolitan style, creative energy, international influence, distinctive way of life and corporate personality . . . to the extent that Los Angeles has these qualities, then to that same extent all the most admired theorists of the present century, from the Futurists and Le Corbusier to Jane Jacobs and Sibyl Moholy-Nagy, have been wrong. The belief that certain densities of population, and certain physical forms of structure are essential to the working of a great city, views shared by groups as diverse as the editors of the *Architectural Review* and the members of Team Ten, must be to that same extent false. And the methods of design taught, for instance, by the Institute for Architecture and Urban Planning in New York and similar schools, must be to that extent irrelevant.

This is a hard thing to say about so many good people who believe that they have the best interests of urban man at heart. Nor can I repudiate their objections with the same absolute conviction they display in their rejections of Los Angeles, because I have been there and know that, while it does indeed perform the functions of a great city, it is not absolutely perfect. I have to admit that I do miss the casual kerbside encounters with friends and strangers to which I am accustomed in other cities – but I am happy to be relieved of the frustrations and dangers of the congested pedestrian traffic of Oxford Street, London. And if it is true that there is no worse form of urban alienation than to be shut up in your own private metal capsule in the abstract limbo of the freeways, I can think of another as bad – the appalling contrast between physical contact and psychological separation in the crowds herded shoulder to shoulder in a public transport system like the Paris Metro where, as Jean Prouvé once told me, '*on a cherché deux heures sans trouver aucun sourire*'. There are as many possible cities as there are possible forms of human society, but Los Angeles emphatically suggests that there is no simple correlation between urban form and social form. Where it threatens the 'human values'-oriented tradition of town planning inherited from Renaissance humanism it is in revealing how simple-mindedly mechanistic that supposedly humane tradition can be, how deeply attached to the mechanical fallacy that there is a necessary causal connexion between built form and human life, between the mechanisms of the city and the styles of architecture practised there.

Consider the implication of this quotation from Herb Rosenthal's report on *A Regional Urban Design Center for the West Coast* (the quotation is in itself a pair of quotations from other sources conflated by Rosenthal):

Already the apartment houses springing up on the edge of Damascus have the look and scattered siting of their Arroyo Seco counterparts, and villas up in the hills beyond Beirut are very similar to the individual houses being built in the foothills beyond San Bernardino. . . . As they burgeon, foreign cities are likely to look more and more like American cities, particularly Los Angeles. The resemblance may be caused more by the automobile as a way of life, than by closer communications . . .

Whatever the original authors of these quotes were arguing, their juxtaposition by Rosenthal tends to confirm the common mechanistic misconception that everything in Los Angeles is caused by the automobile as a way of life. I trust that the preceding chapters will have made it clear that, if there has to be a mechanistic interpretation, then it must be that the automobile and the architecture alike are the products of the Pacific Electric Railway as a way of life.

But all such explanations miss the point because they miss out the human content. The houses and the automobiles are equal figments of a great dream, the dream of the urban homestead, the dream of a good life outside the squalors of the European type of city [122], and thus a dream that runs back not only into the Victorian railway suburbs of earlier cities, but also to the country-house culture of the fathers of the US Constitution, or the whig squirearchs whose spiritual heirs they sometimes were, and beyond them to the *villegiatura* of Palladio's patrons, or the Medicis' *Poggio a Caiano*. Los Angeles cradles and embodies the most potent current version of the great bourgeois vision of the good life in a tamed countryside, and that, more than anything else I can perceive, is why the bourgeois apartment houses of Damascus and the villas of Beirut begin to look the way they do.

This dream retains its power in spite of proneness to logical disproof. It is the dream that appears in Le Corbusier's equation: *un rêve* × 1,000,000 = chaos. Unfortunately for Le Corbusier's rhetorical mathematics, the chaos was in his mind, and not in Los Angeles, where seven million adepts at California Dreaming can find their way around

122. *A Bigger Splash* (oil painting), 1968, David Hockney

without confusion. But since the dream exists in physical fact – as far as it can – its real failings are manifest enough to be well chronicled. But so too is the untarnished dream itself, at least in allegorical form. If Nathanael West's *Day of the Locust* is the most visually perceptive account of its failings to appear in fiction, another locust book, Ray Bradbury's *The Silver Locusts* (The Martian Chronicles) is the purest distillation of the essential dream, in spite of its Martian subject-matter.

The neon-violet sunset light that disquieted the sensibilities of West's hero by making the Hollywood Hills almost beautiful [123], is also the light in which I personally delight to drive down the last leg of Wilshire towards the sea, watching the fluorescence of the electric signs mingling with the cheap but invariably emotive colours of the Santa Monica sunset. It is also the light which bathes Bradbury's Martian evenings. The lithe, brown-skinned Martians, with their 'gold-coin eyes', in Bradbury's vision are to be seen on the surfing beaches and even more frequently on the high desert, where communities like California City sprawl beside shallow lakes under the endless dry wind, and are his Martian ecology to the life. If the famous vision of a totally automated house, that will go on dispensing gracious living long after the inhabitants have vanished, has a prototype in existence it is probably over in Sherman Oaks, and if you seek a prototype of the crystal house of Ylla, look among the Case Study houses or in the domestic work done by Neutra in the fifties.

There is even the unspeakable Sam Parkhill, patented title-holder to half the land of Mars, for all the world like a Yankee 'Don' newly possessed of some vast Spanish rancho; there are the canals by which the crystal pavilions stand, as they were meant to stand in the dream-fulfilment city of Venice; above all, there are the dry preserved remains of the cities of an earlier Martian culture, like abandoned Indian pueblos or the forgotten sets of famous movies long ago . . .

Angeleno Bradbury, sensibilities tuned to the verge of sentiment-ality, touches the quintessential dream in every other paragraph of his

123. *Hollywood* (silk screen print) 1968, Edward Ruscha

Martian chronicles – the exquisitely wrought and automatic houses, abiding for ever in elegant and cultured leisure through the calm of a pluperfect evening 'when the fossil sea was warm and motionless, and the wine-trees stood stiff in the yard'. Tod Hackett, the hero of the *Day of the Locust*, by contrast, is an outsider from the Yale art school, and his eastern sensibilities are outraged by the extravagant styles of the houses he sees as he goes up Pinyon Canyon. Dynamite is the only balm his mind can envisage, until he notices that the houses are all built of ephemeral materials that 'know no law, not even that of gravity' and then 'he was charitable. Both houses were comic but . . . eager and guileless. It is hard to laugh at the need for beauty and romance.'

It is indeed, especially face to face with the physical reality. The distant view, processed through morality and photography, erudition and ignorance, prepares us, as Nathan Silver rightly observed, for almost anything except what Los Angeles looks like in fact. The closer view can be totally disarming, precisely because of that eager guilelessness, that technically resourceful innocence that is in the art of surfing, in the politics of local liberals, and in practically everything else that is worth attention, including most of the Los Angeles architecture of any repute. At its most extreme it can become a naïvely nonchalant reliance on a technology that may not quite exist yet. But that, by comparison with the general body of official Western culture at the moment, increasingly given over to facile, evasive and self-regarding pessimism, can be a very refreshing attitude to encounter.

But there is more to it than technological self-confidence. There is also still a strong sense of having room to manoeuvre. The tradition of mobility that brought people here, sustained by the frenzy of internal motion ever since, and combined with the visible fact that most of the land is covered only thinly with very flimsy buildings, creates a feeling – illusory or not – that you can still produce results by bestirring yourself. Unlike older cities back east – New York, Boston, London, Paris – where warring pressure groups cannot get out of one another's hair because they are pressed together in a sacred labyrinth of cultural monuments and real-estate values, Los Angeles has room to swing the proverbial cat, flatten a few card-houses in the process, and clear the ground for improvements that the conventional type of metropolis can no longer contemplate.

This sense of possibilities still ahead is part of the basic life-style of Los Angeles. It is, I suspect, what still brings so many creative talents to this palm-girt littoral – and keeps most of them there. For every pedestrian litterateur who finds the place 'a stinking sewer' and stays only long enough to collect the material for a hate-novel, for every visiting academic who never stirs out of his bolt-hole in Westwood and comes back to tell us how the freeways divide communities because he has never experienced how they unite individuals of common interest . . . for these two there will be half a dozen architects, artists or designers, photographers or musicians who decided to stay because it is still possible for them to do their thing with the support of like-minded characters and the resources of a highly diversified body of skills and technologies.

In architecture, and the other arts that stand upon the immediate availability of technical aids, the ill-defined city of the Angels has a well-defined place of honour. Any city that could produce in just over half a century the Gamble house, Disneyland, the Dodge house, the Watts Towers, the Lovell houses, no fewer than twenty-three buildings by the Lloyd Wright clan, the freeway system, the arcades of Venice, power-stations like Huntington Beach, the Eames house, the Universal City movie-lots, the Schindler house, Farmers' Market, the Hollywood Bowl, the Water and Power building, Santa Monica Pier, the Xerox Data Systems complex, the Richfield Building, Garden Grove drive-in Church, Pacific Ocean Park, Westwood Village *paseo*, Bullock's-Wilshire, not to mention some one hundred other structures that are discussed in the preceding chapters (or should have been!) . . . such a city is not one on which anybody who cares about architecture can afford to turn his back and walk away without a word further. Such a very large body of first-class and highly original architecture cannot be brushed off as an accident, an irrelevance upon the face of an indifferent dystopia. If Los Angeles is one of the world's leading cities in architecture, then it is because it is a sympathetic ecology for architectural design, and it behoves the world's architects to find out why. The common reflexes of hostility are not a defence of architectural values, but a negation of them, at least in so far as architecture has any part in the thoughts and aspirations of the human race beyond the little private world of the profession.

Towards a Drive-in Bibliography

As the hippie-girls told me, there's lots of picture-books about LA already. Indeed, the bibliography seems to have passed critical mass and to be multiplying explosively of its own accord. In scholarly works, a figure of some 140 to 200 cited sources appears to be about par for the course. Much of this literature is dim, academic, overspecialized, and (mercifully) inaccessible to the general reader. On the other hand, some of what is relatively inaccessible and specialized is extremely rewarding and even interesting, and worth fighting to get. The book-list below therefore makes no distinction between what is easily available and what is difficult; every item is, to my mind, worth pursuing, especially the first.

Los Angeles . . . Zweimillionenstadt in Südkalifornien, by Anton Wagner, Leipzig, 1935.
The only comprehensive view of Los Angeles as a built environment. Wagner had relatives on the vineyards at Anaheim, so his exemplary German scholarship is reinforced by involvement and folk-memory. The result is one of the few works of urban exposition that comes within sight of Rasmussen's *London: the Unique City,* however different its methods of study.

The general history of the city that is usually recommended, again because it is more than one man and one generation deep is
Los Angeles from Mission to Modern City, by Remi Nadeau, New York, 1960.
While those who need to brush up on the history of the State of California at large can still hardly do better than that old war-horse of a college text:

California, by John W. Caughey, Englewood Cliffs (Prentice Hall History Series), 1953, which has the advantage of being written from a UCLA, rather than the usual Berkeley, point of view.

The definitive picture-book is ·
Panorama; a picture-history of Southern California, by W. W. Robinson, Los Angeles, 1953, for which the pictorial material came from the vast and unique photographic collection of the Title Insurance & Trust Company, whose house-historian Robinson was for years. Anything over Robinson's signature or the Title Insurance & Trust imprint can be recommended.

The civic and governmental history of Greater Los Angeles is notoriously complex, but is a prime factor in controlling the form in which it has been built. Two comprehensive but not unwieldy studies are *Southern California Metropolis*, by Winston Crouch and Beatrice Dinerman, Los Angeles, 1963
and
Fragmented Metropolis, by Robert M. Fogelson, Cambridge, Mass., 1968. Behind both stands a classic piece of research:
How the Cities Grew, by Richard Bigger and James Kitchen, Los Angeles (UCLA Bureau of Governmental Research), 1953, but anybody who wants to get most of the worms'-nest of urban problems and civic adventures in one convenient capsule should still turn to
Los Angeles; prototype of super-city, by Richard Austin Smith, *Fortune* magazine, March 1965, even though it now wears a slightly quaint air from having been written in the last months of untainted optimism before the Watts riots.

Before proceeding to specifically architectural studies, it is necessary to draw attention to a particularly Angeleno type of writing that is of tremendous value to any student of the growth and life of the city.

Gossipy and seemingly disorganized, concealing more genuine scholarship than they care to admit and incorporating hearsay and journalism that scholars find difficult to handle, they ramble at seeming random over their subject-matter and contrive to impart vast quantities of otherwise inaccessible information. The prototype of the genre is *An Historical Sketch of Los Angeles County*, by J. J. Warner, Benjamin Hayes, and J. P. Widney, Los Angeles, 1876 (reprinted 1936), which was written while the community was still small enough for everybody to know everybody and remember everything, so that many of the references demand inside knowledge to be understood, but the fresh, eye-witness quality is to be relished. The two major studies in this vein, however, are an encyclopedic funeral oration for the Pacific Electric Railway:
Ride the Big Red Cars, by Spencer Crump, Los Angeles, 1962,
and an enthusiast's account of the rise and middle years of Wilshire Boulevard (good enough to deserve an up-to-date second edition)
Fabulous Boulevard, by Ralph Hancock, New York, 1949.

The freeways, alas, have yet to find either a poet or an historian, but more conventional structures have been better served by the literature. For a start, there is no substitute for
A Guide to Architecture in Southern California, by David Gebhard and Robert Winter, Los Angeles, 1965, which can hardly need futher recommendation, while the 'one-woman crusade' on behalf of Southern California architecture, to which its authors refer, now begins to amount to a respectable body of work, as follows:
Five California Architects, ed. Esther McCoy, New York, 1960,
with essays on Maybeck, Gill, Schindler, and the brothers Greene (this last by Randell Makinson),
and the definitive study of John Entenza's Case Study House Program:

Modern California Houses, by Esther McCoy, New York, 1963,
and a monograph on a single Angeleno architect:
Craig Ellwood, by Esther McCoy, New York, 1968.

Beyond this, the architectural literature is as scattered as it is diverse
(for proof, try to follow up the references in any article by David
Gebhard, most voracious of architectural readers) but the elusive
topic of Spanish Colonial Revival and its 'cognate modes' is well
covered, either by
California's Architectural Frontier, by Harold Kirker, San Marino, 1960,
or
The Spanish Colonial Revival in Southern California (1895 – 1930), by
David Gebhard, *Journal of the Society of Architectural Historians*, XXVI,
2 May 1967.
While Fantastic Architecture, whose Angeleno manifestations are
likely to be as puzzling to outsiders as the Revival, can be approached
by way of
Simon Rodia's Towers in Watts, by Paul Laporte, Los Angeles (Los
Angeles County Museum of Art), 1962,
or
Electrographic Architecture, by Tom Wolfe, (originally published in the
Los Angeles Times magazine supplement, 1 December 1968, as *I drove
around Los Angeles and its crazy, etc.*, but easier to find in) *Architectural
Design*, July 1969,
or
· *The Hollywood Style,* by Arthur Knight and Eliot Elisofon, New
York, 1969, which covers an older type of fantasy,
and for a high-level architectural view of Disneyland:
You Have to Pay for the Public Life, by Charles Moore, *Perspecta*, the Yale
Architectural Journal, IX, October 1964,

Finally, for a view of the typical Angeleno building and environment 'like it is', we have no substitute as yet for the extraordinary picture books assembled by Ed Ruscha, most notably:

Some Los Angeles Apartments, Los Angeles, 1965;

Every Building on the Sunset Strip, Los Angeles, 1966;

and

Thirty-four Parking Lots, Los Angeles, 1967.

Fiction serves the student of Los Angeles almost as well as the student of Paris or London, where topography and townscape impose themselves in a rather similar way. Two items have already been mentioned in the last chapter:

The Day of the Locust, by Nathanael West, New York, 1939, Harmondsworth, 1963,

and

The Silver Locusts (The Martian Chronicles), by Ray Bradbury, 1951 (but the quintessential Martian allegory, *Dark they were and Goldeneyed*, will be found in *The Day it Rained Forever*, by Ray Bradbury, 1959). Much of the fictional coverage of Los Angeles is overtly moralistic and symbolic, notably:

The Slide Area, by Gavin Lambert, London, 1959;

and

Myra Breckinridge, by Gore Vidal, London, 1968.

But a different kind of lost innocence, involving a loss of the *scenes* of innocence, pervades

The Canyon, by Peter Viertel, 1940,

and

The Flashlight, by Eldridge Cleaver, *Playboy* Magazine, December, 1969. Cleaver's story is very much an underworld view of Los Angeles but it is a different underworld from that of

The Big Sleep, *The Lady in the Lake* or *Farewell my Lovely*, by Raymond Chandler (all in *The Raymond Chandler Omnibus*, London, 1962) which in their written form represent the city in the twenties and thirties, and in the form of movies give a now-irreplaceable view of Los Angeles in the forties or thereabouts (and speaking of movies, it is worth remembering that most of the silent classic comedies were shot on real locations in Hollywood, Silverlake, Culver City, etc., and form an archive of urban scenery around 1914–27 such as no other city in the world possesses).

Index